Tranquillizers and Antidepressants

Professor Malcolm Lader is Emeritus Professor of Clinical Psychopharmacology at the Institute of Psychiatry, King's College, London. For 31 years he was an Honorary Physician at the Maudsley Hospital and conducted and supervised clinics dealing with anxiety, sleep and depressive disorders and drug treatment problems. His main research interest is the drugs used in psychiatry, especially tranquillizers and antidepressants, and he has lectured widely and published 20 books and about 650 scientific articles. In addition to advising UK government departments and the World Health Organization, Professor Lader is also a member of various national advisory committees. He is a Fellow of the Royal College of Psychiatrists and of the Academy of Medical Sciences.

Overcoming Common Problems Series

Selected titles

A full list of titles is available from Sheldon Press,
36 Causton Street, London SW1P 4ST and on our website at
www.sheldonpress.co.uk

Body Language: What You Need to Know
David Cohen

The Complete Carer's Guide
Bridget McCall

The Confidence Book
Gordon Lamont

Coping Successfully with Period Problems
Mary-Claire Mason

Coping with Age-related Memory Loss
Dr Tom Smith

Coping with Chemotherapy
Dr Terry Priestman

Coping with Compulsive Eating
Ruth Searle

Coping with Diverticulitis
Peter Cartwright

Coping with Family Stress
Dr Peter Cheevers

Coping with Hearing Loss
Christine Craggs-Hinton

Coping with Heartburn and Reflux
Dr Tom Smith

Coping with Macular Degeneration
Dr Patricia Gilbert

Coping with Radiotherapy
Dr Terry Priestman

Coping with Tinnitus
Christine Craggs-Hinton

The Depression Diet Book
Theresa Cheung

Depression: Healing Emotional Distress
Linda Hurcombe

Depressive Illness
Dr Tim Cantopher

The Fertility Handbook
Dr Philippa Kaye

Helping Children Cope with Anxiety
Jill Eckersley

How to Approach Death
Julia Tugendhat

How to Be a Healthy Weight
Philippa Pigache

How to Get the Best from Your Doctor
Dr Tom Smith

How to Make Life Happen
Gladeana McMahon

How to Talk to Your Child
Penny Oates

The IBS Healing Plan
Theresa Cheung

Living with Autism
Fiona Marshall

Living with Eczema
Jill Eckersley

Living with Heart Failure
Susan Elliot-Wright

Living with Loss and Grief
Julia Tugendhat

Living with a Seriously Ill Child
Dr Jan Aldridge

The Multiple Sclerosis Diet Book
Tessa Buckley

Overcoming Emotional Abuse
Susan Elliot-Wright

Overcoming Hurt
Dr Windy Dryden

The PMS Handbook
Theresa Cheung

Simplify Your Life
Naomi Saunders

Stress-related Illness
Dr Tim Cantopher

The Thinking Person's Guide to Happiness
Ruth Searle

The Traveller's Good Health Guide
Dr Ted Lankester

Treat Your Own Knees
Jim Johnson

Treating Arthritis – The Drug-Free Way
Margaret Hills

Overcoming Common Problems

Tranquillizers and Antidepressants

When to start them, how to stop

PROFESSOR MALCOLM LADER

sheldon PRESS

First published in Great Britain in 2008

Sheldon Press
36 Causton Street
London SW1P 4ST

The author and publisher have made every effort to ensure that the
external website and email addresses included in this book are correct and
up to date at the time of going to press. The author and publisher are not
responsible for the content, quality or continuing accessibility of the sites.

British Library Cataloguing-in-Publication Data
A catalogue record for this book is available from the British Library

ISBN 978–1–84709–023–2

1 3 5 7 9 10 8 6 4 2

Typeset by Fakenham Photosetting Ltd, Fakenham, Norfolk
Printed in Great Britain by Ashford Colour Press

Produced on paper from sustainable forests

Contents

Note to the reader

While every reasonable care has been taken to check information about drugs, particularly dosages, errors may have occurred. Furthermore, dosage schedules are continually revised, indications updated, and new side effects documented. The reader is strongly urged to consult his or her doctor or a pharmacist before taking any unfamiliar medications mentioned in this book.

The standard abbreviations 'mg' for 'milligram(s)' and 'ml' for 'millilitre(s)' are used throughout this book.

1

Introduction: why write this book?

When I was a consultant doctor, many people contacted me because they were worried about trying to stop taking tranquillizers or antidepressants prescribed by their general practitioner (GP) or specialist. Others were concerned about starting such medications because they believed them to be addictive and that they would be condemned to take them every day or night for the rest of their lives. Some were taking their medicines regularly and acknowledged that there was some benefit, but were unhappy about stopping taking them, as advised by their GP, because they feared they would become ill again. Others wanted to come off their medicines but feared they would not succeed because they had heard from relatives, friends or through the media how difficult this could be. And there were others who had tried to stop but had developed unpleasant or even alarming symptoms, even to the point of fearing they were going mad. Others were in the throes of withdrawal, undergoing agonies, and were stuck: they did not want to increase the dose because that would be a backward step, further destroying their confidence, nor could they continue lowering the dose of the medication because they could not face any increase in their distress.

Another group turned to me and my clinical team in desperation because they had struggled through stopping their medicines completely, but had developed distressing symptoms that showed no signs of abating.

Of course, we were hearing from and being referred to people with the worst symptoms. In our extensive research, we had met and identified numerous individuals who wondered what all the fuss was about. They had become depressed or anxious, seen their GP, been correctly diagnosed and, if the condition had been severe enough, had been prescribed an antidepressant or a tranquillizer. This they took for a few weeks or months. They had felt much better. They then stopped their tablets without any real trouble.

Meeting, treating and studying such people raised in our minds a whole host of questions. Why was tranquillizer use and cessation associated with so many difficulties? Were the problems with antidepressants really less? What made one person liable to the tortures of severe withdrawal while another could start and stop these medications with impunity, developing only a few, mild side effects when starting on their pills and showing no signs of withdrawal when they stopped? And most importantly, how could we help all these people?

As well as these practical aspects, we began to think about the wider issues. Was the withdrawal a form of addiction or was it a separate and less worrying condition? Why some medications and not others? Was it worth even considering the use of these medications in view of the problems associated with them? Did we define withdrawal, abuse, addiction in a way that was helpful to individuals who had run into difficulties?

My clinical and research teams were among the pioneers in this area, and our experience dates back to the early 1970s, when we first became aware of the problems associated with tranquillizers and sleeping tablets. But such difficulties had been described years before with older drugs such as the barbiturates and the amphetamines. We referred back to those earlier experiences in order to establish new methods of helping those who came to us, either on their own initiative or referred by GPs or other specialists. We set up individual or group therapy, usually related to so-called cognitive behavioural therapy rather than analytical-based psychotherapy. So did other specialists who started clinics across the country. At the same time, patients themselves set up support and self-help groups. This reflected in part the disillusion of many sufferers with the medical profession. After all, who had first prescribed the medication that was giving them so much trouble? But again, I emphasize that it was a minority of people who needed this degree of help from doctors or their fellow-sufferers. Others took their tranquillizers without complications.

The early clinical experience and research mainly involved tranquillizers, so-called benzodiazepines ('benzos' for short), referring to their chemical structure. The advent of antidepressants with more focused actions on the brain led to concern that similar problems would result from their use. This remains a matter of controversy, and debate continues, often somewhat uninformed. Depression is a more serious disorder than anxiety or insomnia, with greater symptom distress and disruption of work and social functioning; the assumption that antidepressants were as 'addictive' as tranquillizers could lead to depressed people refusing to take their medication as prescribed.

The purpose of this book is both educational and practical. The underlying conditions, anxiety and depression, are described, but in outline (other books by Sheldon Press deal with these topics in detail, for example). The various types of medications are described and put into historical context. Comparisons and contrasts are made with older drugs, and drugs used for different purposes, such as antipsychotics and mood stabilizers. Stimulants and alcohol are touched on, as are illicit drugs. The uses of tranquillizers, sleeping tablets and antidepressants are set against alternative treatments. Should medications ever be used as first-line treatments, or should counselling be tried first? How do these medications act on the brain? Do these mechanisms of action explain the difficulties some patients encounter when they try to stop? When should one try to stop – why not rely on these 'chemical crutches' for the rest of one's life?

Withdrawal occupies roughly the latter half of the book – what it is, whether it differs from use, misuse, abuse and addiction, and whether long-term use is truly addictive, or necessary to treat long-term underlying illnesses such as anxiety, insomnia or depression.

Finally, what are the practical steps in becoming drug-free? It is understandable that the involved reader is tempted to gloss over the earlier chapters to go straight to the later practical ones in the search for relief. However, the earlier chapters provide the basis for understanding the processes of withdrawal and the reasons for various strategies that can be used. Armed with such knowledge, the individual can proceed in a rational manner and not just follow a recipe.

The book ends with short lists of useful organizations and further reading.

I hope that at least some of you will be helped, that you will no longer feel that you are battling alone with horrendous symptoms, that you can stop unnecessary medication, and that you can regain control over your own lives.

But let's start with a fairly typical story:

Ann is a 28-year-old nursery school attendant. She developed symptoms of anxiety and depression about three months after the birth of her first child, Ben. She became increasingly depressed and anxious; she then stopped going out shopping and neglected the flat. Her husband was concerned that she was not looking after the baby properly. Her GP was informed and came to visit Ann, as she had refused to go to his surgery.

He diagnosed postnatal depression with anxiety and agoraphobia. He started her on medication, namely the antidepressant paroxetine (Seroxat), 20 mg a day, and the tranquillizer lorazepam (old name,

Ativan), 1 mg three times a day. After some fluctuations in her illness, it gradually resolved. She began to sleep better, her appetite returned and she took an interest in her baby, her husband and her family. She began to live a more social life again.

After six months the GP told her she had largely recovered. Without further ado, she abruptly stopped her tranquillizer, lorazepam. Within three days of stopping the lorazepam she developed symptoms that alarmed her and soon became worse. She found she could not sleep properly; she felt tense and on edge all the time. She noted that noises appeared very loud; lights were dazzlingly bright and she wore sunglasses even on a dull day. She returned in panic to the GP, who immediately put her back on the lorazepam. He told her to taper it off over six weeks, by a reduction of 0.5 mg every week. The symptoms resolved very quickly and did not return during the tapering.

She was still on paroxetine and decided it was time to stop as she felt so well. This time she consulted the GP and followed his instructions carefully. He switched her to a liquid preparation of Seroxat that she could reduce more conveniently. This she gradually tapered off over 12 weeks. The only problem was a few symptoms, mainly dizziness for a week.

After the second baby she again had some symptoms of depression but refused medication this time. She was treated by an expert counsellor in the practice and learned to cope with the anxious and depressive feelings. These resolved after a few weeks. Since then she has been symptom-free, happy and calm, and functions well at work and at home.

2

Medicines that treat psychological symptoms

Before describing the various disorders that can be treated with tranquillizers, sleeping tablets or antidepressants, I shall outline all the medications that can be used. But first, let me clarify some terms. Doctors and nurses and other health professionals often use the term 'drug', especially when talking among themselves. They use it to mean any substance that is taken to prevent disease, manage or cure illnesses. By contrast, non-professional lay people, the general public, usually restrict this term to drugs of abuse or dependence – 'addictive drugs'. The derogative term 'druggie' thus refers to someone abusing drugs such as heroin, cocaine, amphetamines or barbiturates, on a regular basis, to the detriment of their physical and mental health and of their personal relationships and functioning. The term 'medicine' is more neutral, and can refer to anything taken for therapeutic rather than abuse purposes. Variations include 'medication' and 'medicament'. Remedy is another term, but has implications of cure rather than control of symptoms.

What are medicines used for?

Medicines can play several roles. They can be used to prevent disease. For example, millions of people take medicines called 'statins' to lower cholesterol levels in their blood and help fend off heart disease. Other medicines are used to hold symptoms in check. Insulin is injected to control blood sugar levels in diabetes and prevent coma and eventual death.

Sometimes the medicine has to be taken for the rest of the patient's life, as with insulin. In other instances the medicine is taken for a few days or weeks until the disease resolves or the body's defence mechanisms swing into play. An example of this is giving morphine after a heart attack to control the intense pain until the heart starts to heal the remaining muscle tissue. Medications may be taken to stop further episodes of a recurrent illness. Again, heart disease provides a good example: a small daily dose of aspirin will help prevent further heart attacks. Another type of medicine is a direct curative treatment for an illness – an antibiotic for pneumonia, for example.

As well as these, many medicines are symptomatic remedies. Everyone has taken aspirin or paracetamol for a headache. Often the remedy is only partially effective – an analgesic for back pain, for example. It is important that the person taking the medicine should be clear in her or his mind why the medicine has been suggested. You should ask your doctor why you should take it, what effects you should expect, whether there will be any ill effects and what the alternatives are, both drug and non-drug.

Such questions open up the whole topic of main and side effects. Main effects are the desired therapeutic effects; side effects are un-desirable and, therefore, unwanted effects. For example, the statins mentioned above are very well tolerated. Most people take them regularly without experiencing any ill effects. A small number, unfor-tunately, develop muscle pains and may need to stop taking them. Another form of side effect is the 'idiosyncratic effect'. An example is true allergy to a medicine (or sometimes to the colouring matter in the tablet): the patient is unable to take medicine without breaking out in a rash, or even developing life-threatening swelling of the lips, tongue and throat.

Numerous other important qualities are associated with a medicine. How quickly are its effects felt after taking it (speed of onset of action)? How long does it act (duration of action)? When do its peak effects occur? Can it be given to babies, children, adolescents, the elderly or the infirm? If so, is the dosage recommended for adults the same as for those in these special groups? What if the patient suffers from more than one disease and is taking other medication? Will the medicines interact with each other? Is the medicine safe in accidental or delib-erate overdose? If not, how does one treat the poisoning?

Names of medicines

This can be confusing, even for professionals. Many medicines have numerous names, particularly if they are made by various different manufacturers. Nevertheless, every medicine available for author-ized use in the pharmacy has an 'official' non-proprietary name. It is approved by an international committee and is in use worldwide. It is usually cited without an initial capital letter. Then there are proprie-tary names which are the trademarks of each manufacturer (proprietor) making and selling that medicine. They are named with a capital letter. So, atenolol is the official name for a beta-blocking drug used to treat heart problems and high blood pressure. Its proprietary or trade name is Tenormin and it is made by AstraZeneca. Another medicine, clonidine, has two trade names: Catapres when sold to treat heart problems and high blood pressure; Dixarit when used to prevent migraine attacks. Often a medicine will have only one trade name, which usually indicates that it is still protected by the manufacturer's patent. If it is not so protected, then other manufacturers may step in and produce their own versions. These may be sold under their official names (generic products) or under trade names. Just to complicate matters, a medicine may be combined with one or more other medicines to form compound preparations. Some of these have official names, such as co-codamol (paracetamol and codeine), others only trade names.

Medicines and officialdom

Medicines are available in three main ways:

1 The most freely accessible are 'over-the-counter' medications (OTC): they can be bought in supermarkets, other shops and also in pharmacies. They have been officially judged to be safe, but mistakes have been made: paracetamol was freely available, but was being used in overdoses that caused deaths and liver damage; its sale to the public was restricted to packs of no more than 32 capsules or tablets.

2 Pharmacy medicines are those for which you also do not need a prescription, but they can only be sold in a pharmacy in the presence of a qualified pharmacist. He or she should ask pertinent questions about the advisability of your taking the medicine that you have asked for.

3 The most restricted are prescription-only medicines (POMs). They must be prescribed by a professional, a doctor or dentist, who is registered to do so. She or he has to fill out a prescription in the approved manner. The patient usually takes it to a pharmacy to be dispensed, although a few GPs may still make up the prescription themselves. The pharmacy might be a public (high street) or a hospital pharmacy. If the medicine is available in the pharmacy without a prescription, a considerate GP may suggest buying it there if the cost is less than the prescription charge.

A subgroup of POMs is formed by the so-called 'controlled drugs'. These are subject to prescription requirements of the Misuse of Drugs Regulations (1985). The regulations define the persons who are authorized to supply and possess controlled drugs and under what conditions. The legal requirements relating to these drugs – commonly called 'drugs of addiction' – are complex. It is significant to note that many tranquillizers and sleeping tablets fall into one or other schedule of the Regulations, whereas antidepressants do not. Schedule 1 contains drugs such as lysergide (LSD) that are not used as medicines. Schedule 2 includes diamorphine (heroin), morphine, pethidine and secobarbital (a barbiturate). Schedule 3 contains the rest of the barbiturates, and flunitrazepam, temazepam and meprobamate. Schedule 4 includes the rest of the benzodiazepines, as well as body-building steroids and hormones. Schedule 5 only includes weak preparations and has minimal requirements.

The Misuse of Drugs Act prohibits certain activities by the general public (and doctors). It sets out penalties applicable to different drugs according to the harmfulness attributable to a drug when it is misused. There are three classes:

- Class A contains diamorphine (heroin) and other 'opioids', cocaine, LSD, MDMA ('ecstasy'), phencyclidine and class B substances when prepared for injection.
- Class B contains amphetamines by mouth, barbiturates, cannabis, codeine and weaker 'opioids' (synthetic morphine-like drugs).
- Class C contains meprobamate, most benzodiazepines and body-building substances.

All this can be confusing on first reading, with two classifications, one legal and penal (the Misuse of Drugs Act) affecting everyone, and the other (the Misuse of Drugs Regulations) regulating how doctors keep and prescribe these medicines. We shall deal with some of these medicines later and it may be helpful to return to this section to see where each medicine fits in.

The organization that always seems to be in the news is the National Institute for Health and Clinical Excellence (NICE), which is essentially a cost-effectiveness screen. It cuts across the official licensing of a medicine. Thus, a medication can be licensed by the European Agency for the Evaluation of Medicinal Products (EMEA), but only be available on a private prescription because NICE is not convinced that it is worth its cost to the NHS.

Sources of information

This is a minefield for the unwary. People with access to the internet will use a search engine such as Google to try to find information. Remember that monitoring of internet sites is perfunctory so it is difficult to be sure you are being supplied with balanced information and opinion, or whether the site harbours the blathering of a bigot. Look for apparent official authorization such as the pronouncements of a government organization. Information backed by a reputable university or an international professional association is likely to be reliable. Even so, contentious issues such as dependence may be glossed over because of the difficulty of reaching a consensus.

When I Googled in 'diazepam dependence' in April 2007, I returned half a million hits. I ploughed through the first 100 or so but was not very impressed. Some sites were superficial; others were discursive or polemical web-log ('blog') outbursts of rage and spleen. A few, that I do not care to detail, seemed reasonable – that is, they coincided with my views and prejudices!

People with no access to the internet, often the elderly, the technically inexperienced or perhaps those with difficulty concentrating because of psychological symptoms, may find the local library helpful. Again, be careful to look for official pronouncements, and make sure they are up to date.

Professionals – doctors, dentists, nurses and pharmacists – rely on two sources. The first is the British National Formulary. It is a compact book of over 800 pages, printed on thin paper so it is easily portable. It is drawn up by a joint committee of the British Medical Association and the Royal Pharmaceutical Society of Great Britain. It is updated every six months and sent to most UK doctors. It can be accessed on the internet at <http://www.bnf.org>. It deals with all prescribed products in the UK, and lists their wanted and unwanted effects and costs. It has special sections at the front on guidance to prescribing in children, the elderly, those in palliative care, and information about drugs of addiction as well as drugs and sport. It is meant for professionals and is not easy for a lay person to understand. Despite this, it can lead the concerned lay person to useful information, and a sympathetic doctor may be prepared to help in its interpretation.

The other and more detailed source of information for the professional in the UK is the Data Sheet Compendium. A Data Sheet contains the approved official information about a particular drug, drawn up by agreement between the manufacturer and the licensing authority at the time the latter permits the drug to be marketed. It is updated as necessary – for example, a side effect may become apparent on extensive use, and a warning be added to the Data Sheet. The Compendium is massive, running to over a thousand detailed pages, and is certainly not something a doctor totes around.

Finally, whom can you approach for information? A pharmacist is probably a better bet than a GP. There are thousands of medicines available and a doctor cannot be expected to remember them all. Pharmacists, however, specialize in such knowledge and can point the bona fide enquirer in the right direction. But again, rare reactions can occur that have not yet reached the information sources, so sometimes the whole search for information can be frustratingly time-consuming.

Types of medicine

When this book was being written, the British National Formulary for March 2007 contained 15 sections on different types of medicine acting primarily on different parts of the body. Section 4 deals with medicines used to treat disorders of the central nervous system (brain and spinal cord) – see Table 2.1. Section 4 is also the longest section, and contains all the medicines used in psychiatry and neurology. It also includes medicines such as painkillers and those used to treat obesity, because these also act via the central nervous system. The parts of Section 4 that particularly concern us are:

- 4.1 Hypnotics and anxiolytics
- 4.2 Drugs used in psychoses and related disorders
- 4.3 Antidepressant drugs
- 4.4 Central nervous system stimulants.

Each of the above classes will be discussed as we go on. The hypnotics (sleeping tablets), anxiolytics (tranquillizers) and antidepressants will be described fully in later chapters, but their historical background will be dealt with here.

Hypnotics and anxiolytics

These two groups are summarized together because the distinction between them is artificial. Thus, an anxiolytic (tranquillizer) taken as a single dose before going to bed can help induce sleep; conversely, if a sleeping tablet is broken up and taken in portions during the day, it will lessen anxiety and thus act as a tranquillizer. This substitution of one for the other only applies to the older medicines, the barbiturates and

Table 2.1   Central nervous system medicines in British National Formulary (March 2007)

Hypnotics and anxiolytics
Hypnotics
Anxiolytics
Barbiturates

Drugs used in psychoses and related disorders
Antipsychotic drugs
Antipsychotic depot injections
Antimanic drugs

Antidepressant drugs
Tricyclic and related antidepressant drugs
Monoamine oxidase inhibitors
Selective serotonin re-uptake inhibitors
Other antidepressant drugs

Central nervous system stimulants

Drugs used in the treatment of obesity
Anti-obesity drugs acting on the gastrointestinal tract
Centrally acting appetite suppressants

Drugs used in nausea and vertigo

Analgesics
Non-opioid analgesics
Opioid analgesics
Neuropathic pain
Antimigraine drugs
Treatment of the acute migraine attack
Prophylaxis of migraine
Cluster headache

Antiepileptics
Control of epilepsy
Drugs used in status epileptics
Febrile convulsions

Drugs used in Parkinsonism and related disorders
Dopaminergic drugs used in Parkinsonism
Antimuscarinic drugs used in Parkinsonism
Drugs used in essential tremor, chorea, tics and related disorders

Drugs used in substance dependence

Drugs for dementia

the benzodiazepines. Over the last ten years or so, antidepressants have been used increasingly to treat anxiety, and to a lesser extent insomnia. Furthermore, newer sleeping tablets are becoming available that seem to induce a more natural sleep without the depressant, sedative effects of the older compounds. So the situation is increasingly complex, with all three groups of medicines that largely concern us in this book – tranquillizers, sleeping tablets and antidepressants – becoming intermingled in their usage. But let us start with the tranquillizers.

Tranquillizer classes

Numerous names are bandied about for these medicines, essentially prescribed to lessen anxiety. The earliest term was 'sedative', which originally meant that it lessened anxiety, producing a calming effect. More recently it has come to mean inducing feelings of drowsiness or languor, a state originally called 'oversedation' – the older drugs, such as the barbiturates or chloral, were associated with this unwanted effect. The term 'tranquillizer' was introduced and promoted by the manufacturers in an attempt to encourage people to distinguish between the older sedatives, such as the barbiturates, and the newer introductions, the benzodiazepines.

The main difference is, in fact, greater safety in overdosage of the benzodiazepines, together with a somewhat reduced likelihood of inducing dependence and abuse. Sometimes 'tranquillizer' is qualified by the term 'minor' to distinguish these medicines from the 'major tranquillizers' or antipsychotic drugs, a totally different category. Finally, tranquillizers are, as we have seen, sometimes called anxiolytics – dissolvers of anxiety.

The history of tranquillizers

This provides useful insights. Briefly, the use of medicines to lessen anxiety goes back several thousand years, to the discovery that grape juice or grain mash was fermentable. It resulted in fluids containing alcohol (ethanol) that, among various effects on the brain, could induce feelings of calmness and sleep. We now know that alcohol and medicines such as the benzodiazepines have many properties in common, acting on the same brain structures with similar effects. In the nineteenth century, rather crude drugs were introduced, such as paraldehyde and chloral. At the end of that century came the first of the barbiturates: barbitone (termed 'barbital' in the USA) and phenobarbitone (phenobarbital). Numerous other members of this class were introduced, such as anaesthesia-inducing agents (thiopentone and methohexitone), short-acting secobarbital and medium-acting butobarbital. The long-acting phenobarbital found its main use in preventing epilepsy. It soon became apparent that the barbiturates produced drowsiness, that the anxiety-allaying or sleep-inducing effects soon wore off (tolerance), that physical dependence, withdrawal reactions and abuse were common and that overdoses were lethal. Sometimes the overdoses were deliberate, but in other instances accidental – some well-known figures may have died in this way, such as Marilyn Monroe.

Meprobamate was the first medicine to be introduced in the search for safer alternatives, but was a disappointment as it had most of the drawbacks of the barbiturates.

The really major development was the discovery and introduction of the benzodiazepines. These drugs were originally synthesized in the 1930s but laid aside until the 1950s when their ability to lessen anxiety and to induce sleep was recognized. They are quite complex chemicals and act widely in the brain (see Chapter 7). The first one goes under the tongue-twister of an official name, chlordiazepoxide, with the well-known trade name of Librium. The first of the group to be promoted as a sleeping tablet was nitrazepam (Mogadon). Many others have been developed and marketed, not only as tranquillizers and sleeping tablets but also as muscle relaxants and to prevent and treat epileptic attacks. These drugs have been so successful that they have largely replaced the barbiturates. The most popular was diazepam (Valium), which for many years was the most widely prescribed medication in the world. Their main advantage is greater safety in overdose, but they still induce oversedation and can both cause dependence and be abused.

The main differences among the benzodiazepines relate to their duration of action. This is dependent on many factors, but the main one is the technical attribute, the half-life. This topic is discussed in Chapter 7.

The first benzodiazepine marketed in Europe as a sleeping tablet was nitrazepam, with a long duration of action. Over the past 30 years or so, sleeping tablets have been introduced with shorter and shorter half-lives. An example is temazepam, which was the most popular sleeping tablet for many years. Triazolam (not available in the UK) is even shorter lasting. However, medicines chemically dissimilar from but acting similarly to the benzodiazepines have been developed in the search for safer sleeping pills. They constitute the so-called 'z-drugs' – zaleplon, zolpidem and zopiclone (and eszopiclone in the USA). They have short half-lives and some patients prefer them to the older drugs.

Other medications can be used as tranquillizers and/or sleeping pills. They include the antihistamines, buspirone, clomethiazole and herbal products such as valerian.

Antidepressants

The other group to concern us at this point comprises the antidepressants. Again, the background is complicated. Several substances can be taken to boost psychological functions, the commonest by far being caffeine. Caffeine is defined as a mild stimulant. More powerful stimulants include the amphetamines, methylphenidate (Ritalin) and MDMA ('ecstasy'). Stimulants elevate mood in normal individuals but true antidepressants have no such mood-elevating effect – they only change mood in people who have persisting low mood, i.e. the depressives. Antidepressants have a wide range of other effects, including sedation, dry mouth, blurred vision, nausea and so on. These will be detailed in Chapter 8.

The two main groups of antidepressants are the tricyclic type (TCA) and selective serotonin re-uptake inhibitors (SSRI) on the one hand, and the monoamine oxidase inhibitors (MAOI) on the other. Strenuous attempts have been made over 20 years to distinguish between the SSRIs and the TCAs, but the distinction is a matter of degree rather than a fundamental difference.

History of the TCAs

The historical background to the TCAs is even more convoluted than that of the tranquillizers. The story goes back to the discovery of chlorpromazine, the first of the antipsychotic (neuroleptic, major tranquillizer) medicines used to treat psychoses such as schizophrenia. A similar compound, imipramine, was synthesized but proved ineffective in helping people with schizophrenia. However, a Swiss psychiatrist, Roland Kuhn, followed a hunch that something ought to work in depressed patients and tried imipramine with gratifying success. Imipramine (Tofranil) was introduced into medical practice in the UK in 1959 and gradually became established. Chemically, it had three ring structures (hence the name for the class of 'tricyclic'), although later compounds could have one, two or even four rings. A host of similar compounds were introduced, of which amitriptyline and clomipramine (Anafranil) are the best known. Some produce more sleepiness than others but otherwise they are much of a muchness.

History of the SSRIs

The TCAs all caused a range of unwanted side effects that could be quite troublesome, to the point where some people were reluctant to take any more tablets. Scientists in various pharmaceutical companies realized that most of these side effects resulted from actions on the brain and elsewhere in the body that were not needed for the antidepressant properties. They therefore instigated a search for more selective compounds that were effective antidepressants without having the drawback of many serious side effects. The first one to make any impact was fluoxetine, which became part of folklore under its trade name, Prozac. Several others followed, with only minor differences in therapeutic profiles. The class term was selective serotonin re-uptake inhibitors, describing their selective action on the brain chemical serotonin (also called 5-hydroxytryptamine, '5-HT' for short). Other more selective compounds acting on other brain nerve cell transmitter chemicals were also developed and introduced.

Although originally introduced as antidepressants, it was soon realized that, like some of the TCAs, the SSRIs had effectiveness in helping people with various anxiety disorders and eating disorders. Presently, the SSRIs are becoming the medicines of first choice in anxiety disorders, thereby displacing the benzodiazepines.

History of the MAOIs

These compounds are antidepressants that also act on brain chemicals, but by a different mechanism. In the 1950s, the first one, iproniazid, was noted to raise the mood of depressed patients with tuberculosis. It is closely related to isoniazid, which is still used to treat tuberculosis but has no antidepressant properties. The MAOIs have had some usage, particularly in the UK, but never attained the popularity of the TCAs or the SSRIs. One member of the group, tranylcypromine, can cause true dependence.

Other medications with effects on the central nervous system

As Table 2.1 shows, numerous types of medicine are available for various neurological and psychiatric disorders, but not all are the subject of this book. Nevertheless, a few notes are included below on each group.

Antipsychotic drugs comprise a large and widely used group indicated to treat the symptoms of various types of psychotic disorder, in particular to help people suffering with schizophrenia to control their symptoms. Their history goes back to the 1950s, but new compounds are still being introduced. They are usually taken by mouth but can be injected into a muscle or the blood stream. A special 'depot' form of injection into a muscle, that has a prolonged action, is available.

Antimanic medications are used to control symptoms in episodes of the severe psychosis known as mania, or its lesser form, hypomania. Central nervous system stimulants comprise dexamphetamine, methylphenidate and modafinil. The first has very little legal (licit) usage, but is widely abused in the addiction world. Methylphenidate (Ritalin, Concerta) is being used increasingly in attention deficit hyperactivity disorder (ADHD), and disquiet has been expressed because of this extensive use in children. Modafinil (Provigil) is indicated to treat narcolepsy, an intriguing condition in which the person may suffer irresistible urges to fall asleep or drop to the floor.

Drugs used to treat obesity can either act on the stomach or gut or suppress appetite by an action on the brain. Among the latter, the amphetamines and related drugs have fallen into disfavour because of the dangers of dependence and addiction. This leaves sibutramine (Reductil), which is related in some ways to the TCAs.

Drugs used in nausea and vertigo include the antihistamines, some antipsychotic-type medicines, some drugs that act on serotonin in the gut and brain, and a synthetic drug related to cannabis.

Analgesics, the painkillers, comprise numerous medicines. The weaker ones are compounds like aspirin or ibuprofen. Drugs used to prevent and treat migraine fall into this class. The stronger painkillers are opiate-like and are typically powerful drugs of addiction.

Antiepileptics (anticonvulsants) are used to prevent attacks of one of the types of epilepsy or treat an attack when it comes on. There is some overlap with the benzodiazepine tranquillizers – for example, clonazepam has anticonvulsant properties. Others, such as carbamazepine and valproate, are also used without full official approval to prevent attacks of both mania and depression in people with manic depressive disorder (bipolar disorder – BPD). Valproate is now licensed to treat acute manic symptoms.

Drugs used in Parkinsonism and related movement disorders can also be used to treat the movement disorders induced by the antipsychotic drugs.

Drugs used in substance disorders are a motley collection. Acamprosate (Campral) and disulfiram (Antabuse) are available to help people with alcohol problems maintain abstinence. Bupropion, an antidepressant with unusual properties, can help encourage smoking cessation. Nicotine products can substitute for cigarettes. Opioid dependence may be managed by substituting methadone or buprenorphine (Subutex) or by blocking the actions of diamorphine (heroin) with naltrexone

(Nanorex), or by alleviating the symptoms of withdrawal with lofexi-dine (Britlofex). Drugs used to treat dementia have become available. They act in different ways on the brain pathways that are failing. Medicines include donepezil (Aricept), galantamine (Remityl), memantine (Ebixa) and rivastigmine (Exelen). Their use is controversial: doubts about their cost-effectiveness have led the National Institute for Health and Clinical Excellence (NICE) to issue usage guidelines.

Conclusions

All this must seem very confusing to a lay person, and even profes-sionals may be flummoxed at times. The most important thing to grasp is that there is much overlap between the actions of the various groups of medicines.

Furthermore, as the disorders for which they are indicated are often ill-defined, the use of those medicines is often much more rule-of-thumb than scientifically rigorous.

3

What medications are used for

This book deals with two main types of medication: the tranquillizers/sleeping tablets and the antidepressants. The three main targets for treatment are anxiety, sleeplessness and depression, respectively. There is overlap between these disorders and many people complain of feeling anxious and depressed and being unable to sleep properly. Someone who is taking one of these medications, as discussed in the previous chapter, should have some idea why he or she is being prescribed which treatment. This knowledge helps put problems into perspective, explains the need for the medication but also opens up avenues for considering the use of alternative therapies.

First, it is important to distinguish between symptoms, syndromes and disorders. Indeed, this applies to the whole of medicine. A **symptom** is a feeling experienced by the person (subjective). Examples might include pain, itch, nausea, and what concerns us here: anxiety, sleeplessness and depression. Subjective symptoms are in contrast to 'signs', that is, an objective finding by an observer, such as paralysis, muscle spasm, swelling, redness and inflammation. Often, symptoms are accompanied by signs – for example, depression by a miserable expression, anxiety by muscle tension, sleeplessness by inattention the next day.

A combination of signs and symptoms is called a **syndrome**, which means that several features cluster together. For example, a depressive syndrome may include feelings of sadness, slowness and worthlessness, together with the sufferer appearing to be slowed down, or restless, with a woebegone expression. Syndromes, on their own, are not usually recognized as medical disorders, although they may come close to them.

Disorders comprise complexes of syndromes. For example, panic disorder patients fear certain situations, can become very anxious and panicky in those situations, and may fear dying, or at the least, losing control. They will avoid those situations, which may lead to a phobic state. An agoraphobic housewife will be unable to go shopping unless accompanied by her husband. A person with a depressive disorder will have symptoms of sadness and hopelessness, may experience thoughts of harming himself, may appear slowed down and inert, and his work performance may deteriorate so that employment is endangered, thereby bringing severe social consequences. Disorders are what doctors generally try to diagnose. Various criteria have been set up for various conditions. The World Health Organization (WHO) has, almost from its establishment, been concerned to standardize its diagnostic criteria so that doctors, nurses and others can be sure that they are using definitions that are in use across the health professions, and in all countries. These definitions are updated regularly by the WHO as new disorders are discovered or refined, or ideas change about older conditions. The standard WHO glossary is the International Classification of Disease – Version 10 ('ICD-10'), first published in 1994. It contains an extensive section on mental and behavioural disorders with numerous, different, conditions. Most are called disorders, but a few are termed syndromes. Each is coded with the letter 'F' and a number up to 100, although there are many subcategories. Doctors can examine a patient, make a provisional diagnosis, look it up in the ICD-10 and assign a code number, for example, F.32 (mild depressive) or F.13 (mental and behavioural disorders due to use of sedatives or hypnotics). These data can then be used to compare the prevalences of different disorders across regions, treatment responses and so on.

A distinction is made between systems that are designed to help diagnose, treat and predict the outcome of treatment and those that are used for research purposes. The latter usually have more stringent criteria (the best example is the one drawn up by the American Psychiatric Association – the Diagnostic and Statistical Manual, Version 4 – which has hundreds of disorders, all with claimed differences).

The basic problem with these diagnostic systems is that many, perhaps most, patients have more than one disorder either at the same time (co-morbidity) or in succession over a lifetime. This means that a multiple diagnosis may be needed. It is hardly surprising that many doctors have despaired at these attempts at categorization and harmonization and have adopted a 'problem-orientated' approach instead. This comprises assessing the patient 'in the round', listing the health and social problems and tackling them individually.

Severity

One factor is fundamental to the diagnosis and treatment of illnesses, whether physical (bodily), psychological (mental) or a combination of both. The question that all doctors ask is, 'How serious is the condition?' Typically, three or four grades are used: mild, moderate, severe and very severe. In each condition, different aspects of serious-ness or severity will establish the degree. For example, if a depressed individual only occasionally thinks about having no future, it will probably be ranked a 'mild' suicidal feature; if he thinks quite often about ending it all, the suicidal features are deemed 'moderate'; serious preparations, such as hoarding tablets, will mean the suicidal risk is regarded as 'severe'. A 'very severe' suicidal patient may have made a determined attempt and only survived by a chance intervention. With less crucial symptoms or behaviour each doctor or other health professional will have his or her own calibration scale, but usually some general agreement can be found as to where the boundaries lie. Thus, an agoraphobic patient will be deemed mildly ill if she or he can enter a crowded situation such as a supermarket despite some panicky feeling; moderately ill if some avoidance occurs, such as shop-ping at quiet times; severely ill if the supermarket is only attainable when accompanied by a relative or friend; and very severely ill when the sufferer is completely housebound. Rating scales are available to try to standardize degrees of severity, but most doctors do not use them routinely. In the research context, such as in a clinical trial of a potential new treatment, standard ratings are used. The investiga-tors will be trained to use them, so that there is agreement among them as to the presence and severity of each symptom. For example, the Montgomery–Åsberg Depression Rating Scale has ten items rating various features commonly found in depression. The doctor rates each one on a scale of one to seven within clearly defined categories. The ratings are added up to give a total severity scale. This can be used to ensure that only truly depressed patients are studied, say those with a score of 22 or above, or 30 or more for severe depression; hence rating each patient on successive occasions provides an index of improve-ment or worsening.

As well as these rating scales used by professional observers such as GPs or psychiatrists, some scales are designed to be filled in by the patient herself. Thus, one version of the Hospital Anxiety and Depression Scale comprises 14 questions, seven relating to depressive symptoms and seven to anxiety. There are four grades of severity, and the patient ticks one of the boxes to describe her or his feelings on average over the previous week. Again, the scale can be used to ascer-tain whether the respondent has real depression or anxiety, its degree, and any change with treatment.

Other examples of rating scales are those used to detect and measure any symptoms that emerge when the patient's treatment is stopped.

Interference with functioning

We have dealt so far with how someone with psychological problems feels and how he or she appears. A third feature, which is equally important, is how the person behaves. Has the mental illness impaired functioning? If it has not, then the mental illness may be symptomatically unpleasant but it has no general consequences for the sufferer. But if function is impaired, then the condition has implications beyond the individual.

What are these functions? Generally speaking they fall under one of three headings. First, there is **interpersonal** functioning, which is psychojargon for how the individual relates to other people, primarily his family. Someone who becomes depressed often loses his usual pleasant nature and becomes irritable, subject to angry outbursts. He is on a 'short fuse' and his family tiptoe around him.

Second, **social** functioning may become restricted. The panicky individual avoids stressful situations and her or his social horizons shrink. Contact is lost with friends. Indeed, someone with severe social phobias may become panicky even trying to hold a telephone conversation. Social isolation ensues.

The third sphere of function is the **occupational** one. Jobs, especially challenging ones, require motivation, attention and concentration. These may all be impaired in one way or another. Thus, the depressive cannot bother to go to work, regarding his occupational capabilities as worthless. The anxious individual is so concerned about the possible consequences of all his activities that he cannot attend to matters in hand. The obsessive has disturbing, anxiety-provoking thoughts that plague him and interfere with his concentration.

All of these symptoms, syndromes or disorders can lead to profound functional impairment, often as great as in someone with a severe physical disability. This leads to a general impairment in the quality of life (QOL), a vague concept that, nevertheless, is capable of being assessed. This allows different disorders to be compared right across the spectrum of disease. If all of these functional impairments and QOLs are multiplied by the number of sufferers, the overall burden on society in personal, social and economic terms can be estimated. Mental illnesses, in particular depression, rate highly in this respect. They are serious conditions for people, their families and society.

The borderline between health and illness

Although it would appear that the definitions of illness allow precise diagnoses and appropriate treatments, this is far from being the case. Concepts of normality differ widely from person to person, health professional to health professional and culture to culture. Thus, one person may regard a group of symptoms or an item of behaviour as being within the normal range; another might deem it abnormal. Health professionals will have different concepts of both the type and extent of various symptoms, signs and behaviour. Psychiatrists who have received their training in the same hospital will rate patients more similarly than will psychiatrists trained in other hospitals or other countries. Different cultures will view different behaviours in different ways. What passes for normality or, at most, eccentric behaviour in one group is stigmatized as mentally abnormal in another.

This lack of uniformity has led to accusations that doctors 'medicalize' normal behaviour and find disorders where they do not really exist. In other branches of medicine there are tests that help establish whether a person is ill. For example, blood tests have a normal range for each laboratory, so that people's values outside that range are deemed to be abnormal. An X-ray may show a suspicious shadow. Admittedly, even with supposedly objective tests, controversy may arise. For example, debate continues as to degrees of abnormality with respect to cervical smears. In psychological medicine such aids are few and far between – even the use of rating scales only results in partial precision.

The upshot is that whether a patient is truly a patient or merely on the fringes of what is considered normal is still a contentious issue. If too many mildly symptomatic people are labelled as mentally ill, then certainly some will really be only 'worriers' or 'the miserable well'. Reassurance will be sufficient and will avoid the expense and complications of treatments. On the other hand, if genuinely ill people are excluded because they are regarded as insufficiently ill to be labelled 'patients', some who would actually benefit from medical treatment will be denied it.

Each doctor has his or her own scale for assessing normality, illness and the grey area in between. The use of medication in treatment will reflect this, as will the doctor's assessment of the medication he or she has in mind. If he judges it reasonably safe, he will use it in people who are only mildly ill. If he is worried about the side effects and safety of a medication he will reserve it for the more severely ill, that is to say, those in need of vigorous treatment.

4

The anxiety disorders

Anxiety is an emotion that we all experience. It is a normal part of the response to a situation in which we feel threatened or stressed. It may help us cope with that situation, but if it is severe, persists or seems out of place, it can interfere with everyday life and impair social and occupational functioning (see Chapter 3). Anxiety is also very unpleasant. It comprises a mixture of subjective symptoms, such as nervousness, fear and irritability, and physical effects, such as a racing heartbeat, dry mouth and muscle tension. The person feels that 'something terrible is going to happen' but cannot specify what that 'something' is.

The distinction between anxiety symptoms and disorders (see Chapter 3 for a discussion of these terms) is an important one as it should influence the decision as to whether the individual can be labelled a 'patient' or not, whether particular treatments are needed, and what the outlook for recovery is. If the anxiety is severe and prolonged and cannot be easily explained, particularly when it is accompanied by interference with daily living, it is probably justifiable to regard it as abnormal or clinical. The person in that state needs to be treated in some way, lest his or her quality of life should become grossly impaired.

A whole range of conditions comes under the heading of anxiety disorder. In all of them, both tranquillizer benzodiazepines and various antidepressants have been used to a greater or lesser extent. A major development that should be borne in mind is that, in the UK at least, the tranquillizers are being slowly replaced by the SSRI antidepressants. The reasons for this development will be discussed in Chapter 8. The various types of anxiety disorders are, briefly, as follows.

Generalized anxiety disorder (GAD) is the most common anxiety disorder – about three per cent of the adult population suffer from it at any one time. About one in seven of people consulting their GP have this condition, so it takes up considerable resources. It is a condition of persistent and markedly inappropriate or exaggerated anxiety, with muscle tension, apprehension and heightened alertness (see Table 4.1 on page 24). People are concerned about health, finances, marital situation or their jobs. But many people find it difficult to pinpoint

Table 4.1 Symptoms of generalized anxiety disorder

Psychological	Physical
Feeling keyed up or on edge	Palpitations
Restlessness	Symptoms of overbreathing:
Difficulty concentrating	– tightness of chest
Difficulty relaxing	– light-headedness
Exaggerated startle response	– numbness or tingling
	Sweating
	Dry mouth
	Nausea
	Diarrhoea
	Frequent urination
	Muscular tension, particularly across the shoulders and back
	Trembling
	Headaches

a particular source of concern, and complain of just feeling generally on edge. Other symptoms include fatigue, muscle aches and twitches, trouble swallowing or passing urine, and stomach pain. The condition may come on acutely, almost without warning. It may then come and go, or wax and wane, without ever fully disappearing. It often becomes chronic: the symptoms become entrenched and last for years. It can come on at any age, and the old are just as likely to suffer from it as the young. Some other conditions can be confused with GAD. The most frequent are an overactive thyroid gland, drug-related conditions (including overuse of caffeine) and abuse of amphetamines or cocaine.

The following in outline is a typical GAD history:

Joan is a 28-year-old computer programmer with no children. As a child she felt very concerned in all sorts of trivial situations that would not have upset a less anxious individual. Instead of 'growing out of' this anxiety she became more anxious as an adolescent. She would rehearse all the activities of the day. Eventually she married a man who was equally anxious, but they gave each other a great deal of support. She went to university and obtained a degree in Information Technology.

With support from her husband and other members of her family, in particular her mother, Joan then coped reasonably well. However, when Joan was 26, her mother became ill with breast cancer and died within a year. In her upset, Joan found she could barely cope with any of her usual activities. She developed a constant fear that something dreadful was going to happen. This fear was focused on her concern that any minor ailment that her husband developed would prove fatal. She found that her heart was often pounding, she sweated, and at times found it difficult to speak because of a dry mouth. She also developed general muscular tension and pain in the front of the chest, but realized this was probably something to do with her mother's symptoms in her final illness. She would also have feelings that objects were unreal and far away. The feeling of being on edge continued and became increasingly intolerable. Joan found that she could not concentrate at work because her mind would go blank; she had difficulty getting to sleep worrying about the possibility that she would lose her job because of her ineffectiveness at work.

Eventually she went to see her GP, who diagnosed a GAD. He did not want to prescribe tranquillizers but referred her on to a very experienced counsellor. Joan found great relief in talking about her symptoms and the dread of being left alone to cope without support. Eventually she learned ways of coping with her fears; at present she is still managing without any medication. She sees her counsellor at regular intervals, about once a month.

Panic disorder (PD) is also common. Here the person has panic attacks that are episodes of intense fear or discomfort, accompanied by severe physical symptoms such as palpitations, sweating, shortness of breath, chest discomfort, dizziness and pins and needles in the fingers or toes. These symptoms can be severe and come on so suddenly that the patient may feel his or her life to be in danger. Many therefore present to the Accident and Emergency Departments of general hospitals and, if misdiagnosed, undergo intensive testing to rule out heart or lung disease. Other patients are terrified that they might lose control or go mad. Patients can often remember their early attacks in great detail. They become increasingly anxious in between attacks and often mull over in their minds what happened in earlier ones. They may become quite preoccupied in this way.

Most people with PD go on to develop **agoraphobia**. This is a persistent and irrational fear of a particular activity or situation believed to precipitate a panic attack. Naturally the patient tries to avoid that situation or to be exposed to it as little as possible, or may enter the situation but make sure that means of escape are available. For example, an agoraphobic may visit the cinema but only stay if a seat next to the aisle is available. People with agoraphobia organize their lives around their disability. They may only go out with a companion, or restrict themselves to the vicinity of their home. They may avoid crowded places, escalators or public travel (particularly underground railways). The most severely ill stay at home and may only feel comfortable in one particular room. All the time, otherwise, they have the foreboding that a panic attack may come on.

Here is a short PD history:

> Donald was a successful young accountant. He had passed his examinations with flying colours and was well thought of by his superiors. His parents had divorced acrimoniously when he was 12. One day, as he was driving back from a weekend in the country with his girlfriend's parents, he developed acute palpitations and was convinced that he was going to die. He pulled over to the hard shoulder of the motorway and asked his girlfriend to drive him to the nearest hospital. There he was seen and had an electrocardiograph and some other tests, which were all normal.
>
> Donald returned home and saw his GP. He was referred to a psychiatrist, who made the diagnosis of panic disorder. He was still having frequent panic attacks and was treated with clomipramine. However, this medication made him feel nauseous and he stopped taking it. Very soon he became fearful about leaving his home and going to work. He returned to see the psychiatrist, who changed the medication to an SSRI antidepressant, and started it at a low dose. Gradually his anxieties settled and he was able to move about more freely.
>
> The psychiatrist then started some cognitive behavioural therapy (see Chapter 10). Donald connected the onset of the panic disorder to the demands that his girlfriend was making for them to become engaged. He was not entirely certain that she was the right person for him, and his parents' experiences had made him very cautious. His panics settled down with continuing medication and therapy. After about six months he had returned to normal and the medication was slowly withdrawn.
>
> When he eventually did agree to marry his girlfriend, Donald had one more episode of panic but this quickly subsided. Eventually they got married and he has not had any further symptoms.

Social anxiety disorder (social phobia) (SAD) is an excessive fear of situations in which the person fears that he or she will be under the scrutiny of others or has an excessive fear of acting in an embarrassing way in that type of situation. The most common of these situations are listed in Table 4.2. This condition differs from agoraphobia in that the individual wants to avoid situations of being observed by others rather than the situation itself. An agoraphobic may be reassured in the presence of a companion; a social phobic may be made worse. The social

Table 4.2   Situations evoking social anxiety

- Public speaking or performing
- Eating or drinking in public
- Talking to other people, particularly superiors
- Approaching or dating people
- Using public lavatories
- Speaking on the telephone in the presence of others
- Being introduced to new people
- Being asked personal questions
- Oral examinations

phobia may be tackled and the person appear to gain control of the phobic situation. But even some experienced actors or musicians may suffer from 'stage fright' all their lives.

The anxiety is threefold. First, the individual worries in anticipation of the situation and rehearses all possible eventualities. Next, she may become anxious or panicky in the situation and may try to escape from it. Finally, she will anxiously analyse afterwards what did happen, her reactions and if she coped badly or adequately.

The condition often develops in late childhood, when it appears as shyness, blushing and reluctance to enter social situations. Most shy children do not develop into social phobics, although they may remain uneasy and withdrawn in social situations. If it does blow up into full social phobia, it can become a handicap and interfere with schooling and work, as well as being symptomatically distressing. Alcohol and drug abuse may follow, the sufferer resorting to these substances in order to combat the anxiety. In fact, about one in five social phobics develop an alcohol-related problem; one in five alcoholics also have social phobia. The social phobic may become depressed and desperate, to the point of attempting suicide.

Some lay groups and the media have raised the objection that social anxiety disorder does not really exist: it is merely 'medicalized shyness', and represents an attempt by doctors, especially psychiatrists, to over-diagnose mental illness. This is an unjustified assertion, as attested by the handicaps associated with SAD and the malign consequences, such as alcoholism.

An SAD history:

Colette is a 29-year-old unemployed woman. She had a disturbed upbringing with a single mother who was a heroin addict for some years. Her mother then stopped injecting heroin but still uses cannabis and cocaine on occasion.

Colette was a very shy and anxious child and avoided contact with her mother's friends, both male and female. As she went into adolescence she found that every social occasion caused a great deal of anxiety before, during and after the experience. When confronted with situations in which she had to talk to people, she developed symptoms of blushing and shaking, and had to run out of the room to the toilet. She realized this was an excessive reaction but could do nothing about it. Eventually, she found that alcohol could help her. Before going into any social situation, she would have two or three lagers and one or two shorts. She particularly favoured vodka. When clearly drunk in this way, she could cope with situations that would otherwise be intolerable. Unfortunately, she found that she was drinking more and more alcohol and was drinking outside the fear-inducing situation. She shrugged this off as unimportant.

She has now developed symptoms of severe shaking. When investigated, it was found that her liver function was very abnormal. She has tried to stop drinking but found the anxiety overwhelming.

At present Colette's liver function is still abnormal and it is clear that unless she stops drinking her health will be greatly affected. The possibility of a liver transplant has even been raised but there seems no point until she can control her alcohol intake and in turn her incapacitating social anxieties.

Specific/simple phobias are very common. People are afraid of a whole range of objects or situations. Some are listed in Table 4.3. The person experiences acute panic when confronted by the object or situation and may run away. He takes great pains to avoid the stimulus. I had a patient who had netted all the windows and doors of her house to stop any birds getting in. These phobias usually develop in childhood or adolescence and may persist. Others lessen as the person comes to terms with the phobia. Drugs can be used in treatment – for example, sedatives for those with travel phobia.

Obsessive-compulsive disorder (OCD) is often serious. The person experiences recurrent thoughts or obsessions that are recognized as unwelcome, unpleasant and indeed irrational. He or she tries to put the thought out of mind but cannot, or tries to resist carrying out the compulsion but fails. The individual despairs at the insistent nature of the thought or at the need to carry out the compulsion but is overcome by the mental pressure. The obsessions are recognized as products of the person's own thoughts but still cannot be easily resisted. Typical

Table 4.3 Some specific phobias

- Enclosed spaces (claustrophobia)
- Heights
- Animals – dogs, snakes, insects, spiders, birds, mice
- Blood or injury
- Storms and lightning
- Going to the dentist
- Air travel
- The number 13

obsessive thoughts and compulsions are listed in Table 4.4. Everyone has had some repetitive thoughts or indulged in checking behaviour at some time; it is only when it becomes excessive that it becomes a mental disorder.

Table 4.4 Some typical obsessive thoughts and compulsions

Obsessions	Compulsions
• Fears of contamination • Excessive doubts • Excessive slowness • Upsetting thoughts (such as of harming people)	• Repeated washing (Lady Macbeth syndrome) • Repeated checking (such as gas taps)

The obsessions can become very time-consuming. One patient I knew spent three hours every morning showering and putting on her makeup before she could leave for work. To make it worse, when she got home she spent two hours taking her makeup off again and continually washing her face. OCD may have a physical basis on occasion – brain inflammations or head injury may leave the individual with obsessive–compulsive behaviour.

Post-traumatic stress disorder (PTSD) is another serious anxiety disorder. It is a reaction to exposure to a life-threatening situation or event that involves oneself or others. The immediate response is intense fear, helplessness or horror. The commonest causes are crime and natural or man-made disasters such as earthquakes, tsunamis, plane crashes and fires. Symptoms are often severe (see Table 4.5 on page 30) and can lead to panics.

PTSD usually develops soon after the traumatic event as an acute condition with great distress, loss of one's bearings and even dissociation, i.e. acting as if in another context. War situations tend to result in more severe symptoms that can be particularly difficult to treat.

Table 4.5   Symptoms of PTSD

- Feelings of guilt about having survived the catastrophe while others have not
- Sleep disturbances such as nightmares and waking up in a sweat
- Heart pounding, dry mouth, excessive sweating
- Recurrent and intrusive distressing recollections of the event
- Feeling as if the event was recurring
- Intense anxiety and panic when confronted with things that remind the patient of the event
- Persistent avoidance of the site of the event or the situation
- Irritability, difficulty in concentrating
- Being overvigilant, liable to startle easily
- 'Flashbacks' – an action replay of the events in the imagination

PTSD is often accompanied by depression, other anxiety disorders and substance and alcohol abuse. Bodily complaints are a particular problem and may dominate the clinical picture.

People exposed to severe trauma commonly develop an acute stress reaction, with anxiety, insomnia and avoidance. Only a minority go on to full-blown PTSD. It is customary to 'debrief' an individual after a trauma, i.e. go over the events and the person's reactions in detail. The bulk of the evidence from careful scientific studies shows that this may actually make some individuals more likely to develop PTSD, rather than prevent the progression. It may be that debriefing causes some people to mull over the event and prevents them from coming to terms with it.

Anxiety as a symptom of other disorders

A number of other psychiatric conditions are associated with anxiety symptoms. Depressive illnesses often contain a major element of anxiety. This may obscure the underlying depression. Schizophrenics in their initial stages may be very anxious because of the other strange symptoms they experience.

Substance abuse, particularly of the amphetamines and cocaine, often produces excessive anxiety. Alcohol can be associated with anxiety when taken regularly in excess. More importantly, anxiety can become severe when overuse of alcohol is abruptly stopped, which may usher in a bout of delirium tremens (DTs).

Of course, any medical condition that is serious, or that the patient believes to be serious, will give rise to anxiety about the future; this may well be justified. But some people worry about trivia and become obsessed with their symptoms (hypochondriasis).

A whole range of medical conditions can be associated with anxiety symptoms. Some of the more common are shown in Table 4.6.

Table 4.6   Some medical illnesses that can cause anxiety symptoms

Cardiovascular	*Neurological*
Heart irregularities	Epilepsy
High blood pressure	Migraine
Angina or a heart attack	Continued and severe pain
Heart valve problems	Multiple sclerosis
Heart failure	Huntington's disease
	Some forms of dementia
Respiratory	*Other*
Insufficient oxygen	Peptic ulcer
Blood clot in the lung (embolism)	Ulcerative colitis
Glandular	
Overactive thyroid	
Overactive parathyroid	
Overactive adrenals	
Tumour of the adrenals	
Menopausal symptoms	

5

Sleep difficulties

Sleep is a major part of our lives. We spend a third of our lives asleep and yet we know little about it. We are unsure why we need to sleep, how many hours are 'normal', and what the consequences are of disrupted, insufficient or unsatisfying sleep. We all know, nevertheless, how unpleasant this can be, whether we inflict it on ourselves or whether it seems to be spontaneous sleeplessness, i.e. insomnia.

Sleep can be defined as a recurring state of inactivity accompanied by loss of awareness and a decreased reaction to the environment. This inattention can be quite selective, as when a mother wakes up instantly her baby cries. For years sleep remained an enigma, but modern scientific techniques, such as all-night recordings of the electrical brainwaves (sleep EEG), have begun to give us useful insights. Basically, sleep can be divided into rapid-eye movement (REM) sleep, in which the eyes swivel from side to side and some bodily functions such as the heart and sweating are active and dreaming takes place, and non-REM sleep, in which bodily functions are quiescent. Non-REM sleep can be further divided into four levels, each with different patterns of brainwaves.

Healthy people go to sleep quite rapidly and their sleep patterns steadily deepen. After about 90 minutes, an episode of REM sleep switches in, lasting 5–30 minutes. Four to six such stages occur during the night, getting steadily longer. Deep sleep is concentrated into the first part of the night. Elderly people usually sleep less than when they were young, both in terms of duration of sleep and its depth. Conversely, children sleep longer than adults and have more deep sleep.

Insomnia

Sleeplessness is a common complaint. Detailed enquiry often reveals that the complainer feels 'tired all the time' during the day, attributing this to poor sleep of one kind or another. Usually this is a realistic appraisal of the situation, but sometimes the individual has unreal expectations. For example, as a person ages he or she may still expect to sleep throughout the night, or take a nap after lunch and still expect to sleep well that night.

Sleeplessness can be divided into whether or not there is an apparent cause – primary as opposed to secondary – or whether the insomnia is transient, short term or long term. Transient insomnia, such as jet lag, lasts only a few nights; short-term insomnia lasts a week or more and is a response to stress; long-term goes on for weeks, months or even years. I will discuss secondary insomnia first, where a probable cause can be detected. That still leaves a large number of insomniacs in which the cause is baffling.

Secondary insomnias

These can be divided into those associated with medical conditions, those related to psychiatric illnesses and those caused by medication or abuse of illicit drugs. Yet others follow psychological factors or unsuitable sleeping conditions. Some of those causes most commonly encountered are listed in Table 5.1 (page 34). The primary way of dealing with the problem is to try to minimize the discomfort caused by one or more of these factors.

Primary insomnia

This form of sleeplessness is diagnosed when none of the above causes seems to be operating. The person just seems to be a 'poor' sleeper. In all cases, the next day the person feels tired but not necessarily sleepy. Three aspects are described:

1 The person complains that he takes a long time to fall asleep, typically more than 30 minutes. He tosses and turns and checks the clock ever more frequently and becomes more and more anxious. Once asleep, he tends to stay asleep.
2 The person falls asleep fairly readily but then wakes up after a few hours and may spend some time falling asleep again. Eventually, the person wakes early and cannot fall asleep again and is awake until she judges it time to get up.
3 The times of sleep seem fairly normal but the person wakes up and does not feel she has had a good night's sleep. This persists into a sense of tiredness the next day.

Mixed patterns are often encountered, with delayed onset of sleep, frequent awakenings and then waking early and unrefreshed. All these types of insomnia tend to persist, but may vary substantially from night to night. A bad night's sleep may be followed by a better night or vice versa. The individual may become overaware of the sleep pattern or even phobic of not falling or staying asleep. This then constitutes a secondary stress, so that the insomnia becomes self-perpetuating.

Table 5.1 Some conditions and substances associated with complaints of insomnia

Medical conditions	
Cardiovascular	– heart failure, angina
Respiratory	– breathlessness at night, asthma, obstruction of the airways
Stomach and gut	– peptic ulcer, diarrhoea
Kidneys and bladder	– enlarged prostate, inflammation of the bladder
Neurological	– Parkinson's disease, Alzheimer's-type dementia; pins and needles, tinnitus (constant buzzing in the ears)
General	– pain, itchiness, arthritis

Psychiatric conditions	– anxiety, depression, mania

Sleep conditions	– late-night eating
	– late-night exercise
	– overstimulation, such as watching a horror film, noise
	– abnormal rhythms, such as shift-work or jet lag

Psychological factors	– stress, tension, grief, abnormal concern about sleeping that sets up a vicious cycle
Medicines and other substances	– caffeine, nicotine, amphetamines and other stimulants
Prescription medicines	– steroid compounds, some beta-blockers, some SSRI antidepressants
Withdrawal from	– alcohol, benzodiazepines, antidepressants

Often, if the story is traced back, it becomes apparent that the individual has always been a poor sleeper. As ageing progresses, the natural changes outlined above make the sleep increasingly unsatisfactory, until the person self-medicates or seeks professional advice from a doctor or pharmacist. In other instances, a woman, say, will attribute her difficulty sleeping to the years she had young children who regularly disturbed her sleep. Later, firm sleep patterns never seemed to re-establish themselves.

Primary versus secondary insomnia – two histories

First, primary insomnia:

Kenneth is a 60-year-old retired capstan-lathe operator. He remembers finding it difficult to go to sleep as a child, and as an adult was always the first to wake up in the household but never felt he had had a full, satisfying night's sleep. He gradually noted that his sleeping had become worse and worse over at least 20 years. He could get to sleep reasonably quickly, but woke several times in the night and found that he tossed and turned for some time until he fell asleep again.

His doctor told him that he was not depressed but that he was suffering from an inbuilt inability to sleep properly. He suggested taking sleeping tablets, at least intermittently, but Kenneth flatly refused to take medication of any sort. He searched the internet and located a therapist who claimed to be able to treat insomnia. The consulting room was nearby so he went round to find out about it. The treatment comprised deep relaxation exercises and seemed at least to have some rational basis for its effectiveness. He tried a few sessions and noted that he did in fact stay asleep for longer and woke feeling more refreshed. He was also told to go for an evening walk, which helped him feel relaxed when he went to bed. He has not taken any medications.

Next, secondary insomnia:

Kay moved to the west of London. She had been reassured that she was not under the flight paths to Heathrow Airport but found that this was not strictly true. There were times when planes would bank over the house and were quite noisy. She found that she was being woken in the early morning by the first flights into Heathrow from the Far East. An expert installed double glazing of the right type. The noise became very much less; she is not disturbed by the planes and now sleeps well again.

Other causes of sleeplessness

Sleep is a complicated state that results from the interaction between inbuilt sleep rhythms and cycles and learned habits. Most people have a series of activities that they carry out routinely when they prepare to go to bed. This is actually a series of acts that serve to put the person in the right physical and mental state to fall and stay asleep. Some people read a chapter of a book; others have a milky night-time drink. Others believe that an alcoholic nightcap does the trick. These habits are often acquired over several years in childhood and adolescence, and last a lifetime. Nevertheless, some people learn bad habits that are known actually to hinder falling and staying asleep. Sometimes, too many activities are carried out in the bedroom, with loud music playing or vivid television programmes. The bedroom can then become associated in the individual's mind with overactivity, not underactivity. These habits need to be addressed and broken (see Chapter 10 for hints on sleep hygiene).

Some forms of insomnia are related to disturbed day–night ('circadian') rhythms. Shift-workers, of whom there are many, often find it difficult to adapt to unusual hours, and insomnia results. Totally blind people receive no visual cues as to whether it is day or night and their sleep rhythms may suffer.

Adolescents and young adults who lead time-chaotic lives make up a group that may develop sleep disorders. They go to sleep at greatly varying times and may get up to no fixed patterns. Sleep rhythms may be disturbed.

Finally, some conditions related to sleep may, in themselves, disturb the sleep rhythms. In nocturnal myoclonus, the patient's muscles jerk uncontrollably, waking her up. Restless-legs syndrome comprises uncomfortable sensations in the legs, such that the patient feels compelled to move them. In obstructive sleep apnoea, the breathing passages may be narrowed. As the patient sleeps, the muscles around the breathing passages – for example, in the back of the throat – become lax, flop forwards and block respiration. The patient stops breathing and then wakes up struggling for breath. A bed partner will report strident snoring between the interruptions of the breathing. The individual may wake up many times during the night, has no recollection of these episodes, but complains of feeling tired the next day. Obstructive sleep apnoea is most common in overweight men, and is becoming more of a problem as obesity increases.

6

Depression

The term depression is a general one, meaning a lower area – for example, a depression in a landscape. In medicine and psychiatry it has a confusing multiplicity of meanings, from an emotion to a severe psychiatric disorder. Let us examine this range.

Depression can be a transient mood; that is to say, we all feel miserable from time to time, usually because of some bad news. Some people, by contrast, fluctuate in mood without obvious cause, being down in the dumps one day and normal or even elated and high the next.

The mood can become persistent, leading to day after day of feeling miserable, but this falls far short of being a mental disorder. Some people are notorious for being permanently miserable, always seeing problems everywhere and complaining about everything. They may not be fun to be with, but they are not usually regarded as mentally ill. Sometimes they can switch over into the opposite mood and be cheerful, optimistic and helpful; sometimes their moods fluctuate with the seasons, happy in summer, downcast in winter. These mood changes are outside the individual's control, and he or she learns to live with them.

Depression can be a symptom, either itself or as a reaction to other conditions. Such depression is understandable in the light of the person's physical health – people told that they have cancer will almost inevitably feel hopeless and depressed. But some illnesses are clearly connected to physical conditions, and not just as a psychological reaction. We have all felt abysmally miserable following a bout of influenza. Other rarer infections can be associated with depression, such as brucellosis, caught from cattle. Conversely, some infections can cause unwarranted heightened mood – think of those well-known fictional depictions of the heroine suffering from tuberculosis, for example, and how she is often portrayed as unduly optimistic.

Most commonly, depression occurs as an illness on its own, rather than as a reaction to another physical illness. The major groups are unipolar disorder, where the patient suffers only bouts of depression, and bipolar disorder, where episodes of abnormally heightened mood occur as well. These attacks are called 'mania' or, in a milder form, hypomania ('hypo' meaning under).

Psychological symptoms

Even mildly depressed patients have an air of prevailing sadness that betrays the lowering of mood. They are miserable, despairing and despondent, and jaded in their spirits. At first, the depressive can put her or his miseries out of mind, particularly when with others or occupied doing interesting work. But if the illness takes hold, the despair and preoccupations with the worst aspects of life come to predominate at all times. Depressives are easily moved to tears, and more seriously depressed people find themselves weeping uncontrollably, though even after 'a good cry' they may still feel depressed. They are inconsolable, and are not helped by sympathy.

One must realize that true, clinical depression is way beyond the normal miseries and worries that we all have experienced at some time. The mood is one of anguish with an indescribable intensity and persistence. All of the person's mental functions are affected. Indeed, at the most severe depths, even patients' ability to feel any emotion is affected, so that they deny feeling depressed but instead describe a complete emptiness of emotional experience.

Depressed patients feel worthless and suffer intense guilt, mulling over in their mind past events, real though usually exaggerated, but sometimes imaginary ('delusions of guilt'). They believe they have failed themselves and let their families down. They ruminate over trivial matters, blowing them up out of all proportion, always making things out to be much worse than they really are. The more severely ill patients will confess these shortcomings to their families, friends and workmates, and even beg forgiveness.

Depressed patients become unsociable and shun social situations that they previously enjoyed. Many patients develop paranoid states, becoming secretive, suspicious and blaming others, rather than themselves, for being in that state. The paranoia may become very intense, the patient believing he is being persecuted by his neighbours or by foreign agents.

A common complaint, and one of the first to be noticed, is lack of energy. Every routine task becomes a major chore. At work, patients lack enthusiasm for their work and quickly become bored. Tasks are avoided or postponed, and this procrastination is accompanied by lack of confidence and indecisiveness. At home, a housewife no longer bothers to cook meals but depends on opening tins and using the local takeaway. Loss of attention, motivation and concentration can be very noticeable, both to the depressed person and those around. Colleagues complain that he is not pulling his weight; at home other members of the household regard all the responsibility as falling on their shoulders. Depressives neglect themselves, particularly with respect to personal hygiene. Women stop using makeup or apply it in a slapdash way, or dress in drab clothes. The self-neglect can reach the point where the patient loses a lot of weight, looking like a scarecrow in clothes several sizes too large.

A very characteristic symptom concerns patients' ability to experience pleasure and joy. They no longer take part in activities that they previously found pleasant and rewarding: the doting grandmother looks forward to the visits of her boisterous grandchildren with dread rather than pleasure; the keen football fan no longer goes to matches and doesn't care whether his team is promoted or relegated. Favourite music loses its appeal, travel its allure. Perceptions become dulled, colours pale and time drags by – an hour seems a day, a day an eternity.

The most upsetting aspect is the possibility of the depressed person becoming suicidal. This is a great worry for family, carers and medical personnel. Suicidal thoughts, preoccupations, tendencies and plans increase roughly in parallel with the depth of depression. Definite stages can be seen, which are reversed as the patient responds to treatment. First, the future seems grey, increasingly gloomy and unappealing. Next, the patient cannot see any future, just existing from one day to the next. He wishes he had never been born and does not really care whether he lives or dies. One patient said to me, 'Just let me fall into a deep sleep; I don't care if I don't wake up.' As the patient may blame himself for all sorts of sins, it seems that killing oneself is the only way out. At first such suicidal thoughts are intermittent, frighten the patient and are resisted. Then they become more insistent – suicide seems to provide the only logical solution. Next, the patient ponders over how to commit suicide: she may hoard her tablets or buy a rope. Impulses to commit suicide become stronger and may dominate the depressive's mind. A rehearsal may be mounted. But often the patient lacks enough interest and motivation to be capable of positive action. The danger point is, ironically, early on in treatment – the patient may still feel very depressed, but through the treatment regain motivation and capability.

A few patients become psychotic – that is, they lose contact with reality. They hear voices that are not there ('auditory hallucinations'), become deluded, with fears of persecution, or may hear voices telling them to kill themselves. Committal to hospital becomes imperative to prevent the patient harming herself or himself and others. The most tragic, but thankfully rare, cases are where a father or mother becomes convinced he or she has led an evil life, and that his or her family will be punished. To save the wife or husband and children from that fate, he or she kills them and then commits suicide.

Bodily symptoms

As well as these profound psychological disturbances, a range of bodily symptoms can be experienced. Of these, sleep disturbances are the commonest. Some anxious, depressed patients find difficulty going off to sleep, but most depressives complain of broken sleep with frequent awakenings, together with waking early. Sleep is lighter and dreams are gloomy and disturbing. About ten per cent of depressives, usually younger patients, oversleep, almost as an escape from their waking miseries. Sleep disturbance can usher in depression.

Appetite is also disturbed. A few people overeat (comfort feeding), but most lose their appetite and weight loss follows. Looseness of clothing is quite a good estimate of the severity and duration of the depression.

Sexual disturbances are early signs of depression and include loss of sexual desire in both sexes, frigidity in women and impotence in men. Menstruation may become scanty or periods may even stop.

Physical symptoms can begin or existing ones become worse. Elderly patients in particular may develop dry mouth, indigestion and constipation. Other symptoms include palpitations, trembling, frequent trips to the loo, breathlessness and sweating. Pain is a very common complaint, headache, lower back pain and widespread rheumatic twinges being commonest. Some pain can be very severe, and be given the term 'neuralgia'. The depressive can become preoccupied with pain and develop a hypochondriacal state. The patient fears that he or she has developed cancer or an incurable disease and is not reassured, no matter how many physical investigations, such as blood tests and X-rays, are carried out. If chronic pain is already present, it becomes more intense, more frequent, longer lasting and upsets the patient more. Attendances at the GP's surgery become more frequent. From this, the astute doctor may diagnose possible depression.

Patients may slow down or become agitated, or even alternate between the two. I have seen patients who could hardly crawl out of bed in the morning, yet by the evening were panicky and restless. The facial expression can be a giveaway. It is fixed in careworn lines with deep furrows in the forehead. Responses to questions can be delayed, and spontaneous speech may not be forthcoming.

Types of depression

The descriptions above apply mainly to more severely ill patients. Depressive severity covers a wide range, from people who are just a little depressed but definitely feel abnormal in themselves, to those in whom depression is a life-threatening illness, with profound loss of weight or serious risk of suicide. Most patients are only mildly ill, some moderately ill and a few very ill indeed. The appropriate treatment is usually chosen on the basis of the severity, and medication is often reserved for the moderately and severely ill.

Another distinction is between those in whom the depression appears to follow a stressful life event, usually of loss, such as the death of a close relative, redundancy from a satisfying job or the breakup of a long-standing relationship. But in some patients, despite careful enquiry, no such cause can confidently be found – the depression appears to arise from within the person. This is the so-called 'reactive/ endogenous' distinction. In most depressives, some sort of stress seems to have activated a predisposition in the individual to respond with a depressive illness.

Depression can come on at any age. Even fairly young children may show symptoms of misery, adolescents certainly. Some people experience their first attack of depression as young adults. This may go away and it may be many years before another attack occurs. Depression may follow childbirth – post-natal or 'puerperal' depression. It was thought that the menopause was a time of particular risk for women, but this idea has lost favour. It is clear, however, that the elderly are particularly prone to becoming depressed. This is partly due to the stresses of old age, such as financial constraints, bereavement, loneliness and physical illnesses, but it is probable that people become more depression-prone as they age.

Other subtypes of depression include:

1 *recurrent brief depression*, in which the attacks of depression last for only a week or two, but recur throughout life;
2 *seasonal affective disorder*, in which there is an annual pattern to the mood changes, depression being commonest in autumn and winter;
3 *atypical depression* – this just means that the illness has an unusual symptom pattern. Anxiety, panics and phobias are common; bodily symptoms may predominate and obsessions worsen.

Mild versus severe depression – two histories

Mild depression:

> Alfred is a 40-year-old plasterer. Recently he suffered a series of bereavements, including a brother, both parents in quick succession and his faithful dog. He became quite upset and felt that life had dealt him a poor hand. He also became somewhat anxious and wondered whether he too would be dying soon. He developed some physical symptoms, including muscle tension, and found it difficult to go to sleep. When he saw his GP, he was offered a tranquillizer but refused to take it because he did not feel it would help; and he was worried about becoming 'addicted'.
>
> Soon after, he talked about his symptoms with a sister, who admitted that she also felt very much the same at times. She had dealt with the depression by taking up long-distance running, and her symptoms gradually went away. Alfred went back to his GP, who was scathing of the idea that exercise would help. Despite this, Alfred took up cycling. He found it very restful because he found a cross-country track, a disused railway line, along which he could cycle without worrying about the traffic. Gradually he recovered and is now back to normal.

Severe recurrent depression:

> Penny is a 55-year-old nursing sister. She had an uneventful childhood and adolescence, married at the age of 25, had two children and settled into a rewarding routine of child care and part-time work as a theatre sister in the local hospital.
>
> At the age of 45 she began to feel that life had lost its pleasures. She could not understand this and was upset by her inability to feel for the family. She found going to work a chore, particularly when on shifts. She became irritable and started to row with her husband, something that had not happened frequently before. Her two boys commented on the change in her personality.
>
> She lost her appetite and her weight decreased by eight kilos (nearly one and a half stone). Her sleep became very fragmented. She began to experience the feeling that life was not worth living and became frightened that she might lose control of herself. She consulted her GP, who referred her as an emergency to a psychiatrist. She was immediately placed on an antidepressant, but it was a week or two before she noticed any change. She began to sleep better but the thoughts of harming herself hardly altered. Because of this she was taken into the hospital for two weeks until she felt appreciably better. She was then discharged on medication and gradually returned to normal.

Since then Penny has had two further attacks of depression, each one getting more severe. She now recognizes when an attack is coming on and immediately returns to see the psychiatrist who first treated her. She has been advised that because the risk of relapse is so great, she should stay on medication indefinitely and not try to withdraw. While on medication she manages to work, but has days when she doesn't feel quite right. She has lost her irritability, but her sleep rhythm has never quite returned to normal.

Bipolar affective disorder (manic-depressive illness)

Earlier we saw that these mood disorders can follow the pattern of recurrent depression only, or episodes of mania can also occur. The manic episodes can come on before the depressive attacks, alternate with them or, most uncommonly, come on later in life. Mania is far less common than depression, so that bipolar disorders only total about a tenth of depressive illnesses.

Antidepressants and other treatments are used to treat the episodes of depression in bipolar patients. The general approach is about the same, although specialists are aware of some difference. Particular care must be taken when treating depressed bipolar patients with antidepressant medication, to avoid pushing them over into mania.

7

Tranquillizers and sleeping tablets

Let us now look in detail at the classes of medication that concern us. It is simpler to discuss these medicines together as there is much overlap between the two. So, if a tranquillizer/sedative is given in small doses two or three times a day, it will allay anxiety throughout this time. But if a larger dose is taken before going to bed, it will help the individual go off to sleep. Nevertheless, each medication of this type is usually marketed by the pharmaceutical company as either a tranquillizer or a sleeping tablet. By far the largest class of drug in these groups is the benzodiazepines (sometimes 'benzos' for short), the term describing their complex chemical structure. In order to understand the immense popularity of these medicines and the problems this caused and is still causing, we must look briefly at their predecessors, the barbiturates.

The barbiturates

People have always sought help lessening their anxieties. The use of chemical substances to this end has long taken place. By far the oldest and most widely used agent has been, and still is, alcohol. But starting in the mid-nineteenth century, chemicals were introduced, such as chloral and paraldehyde. This process culminated in the discovery of the barbiturates just over 100 years ago.

The first one was barbital, which was soon followed by phenobarbital, a long-acting sedative agent used to lessen anxiety but also very extensively to prevent epileptic attacks. At least 50 others followed, of which the best-known are amobarbital (Amytal) and quinalbarbital (Seconal), of medium duration of action. Thiobarbital (Pentothal) is a short-acting medication still widely used to put people deeply asleep before and during surgical operations. Thus, the effects of barbiturates range from preventing epilepsy through mild sedation to general anaesthesia.

But in higher doses, the barbiturates can cause breathing to be depressed, and if sufficient is given, or taken as an overdose, this can result in death. Some people become confused and disorientated after the first dose or two, and continue to take further doses, resulting in accidental death. This is particularly hazardous if alcohol is taken at the same time. As little as ten times the anti-anxiety dose can kill a person; even less if they are intoxicated with alcohol.

Barbiturates can react with drugs other than alcohol. They affect enzymes in the liver that break down other drugs so that their concentration in the body may be increased or reduced. This can result in side effects or loss of effectiveness respectively.

Many adverse effects of the barbiturates affect brain functioning. Slurred speech, blurring of vision and unsteadiness are common. Sometimes, the person becomes overexcitable or irritable and aggressive. In the elderly, confusion and memory problems are hazards. On longer-term use, the barbiturate can build up in the body ('cumulate'), so that the individual becomes slowed down, unable to concentrate, with severe loss of memory and impaired judgement. Some become unpredictably overactive.

The effects of the barbiturate may wear off (tolerance), so that the patient takes increasing doses. Signs of barbiturate intoxication ensue – excessive sleepiness, slurred speech and staggering gait. On stopping the medication, one or more types of withdrawal features can occur.

For all these reasons, the barbiturates had fallen into disfavour by the middle of the twentieth century. Other substances were introduced, such as meprobamate and clomethiazole. These in turn were found to have most of the drawbacks of the barbiturates, and were largely discarded – a process greatly accelerated by the advent of the benzodiazepines.

The benzodiazepines

The background to these tranquillizers was set out in Chapter 2. We noted that they replaced the barbiturates because they were safer in overdosage, interfered less with other medicines taken at the same time and seemed to be unlikely to cause dependence and addiction. The first two of these advantages have been borne out over time, but not the third.

How the body deals with benzodiazepines

We saw earlier how the body gets rid of medicines, usually by breaking them down in the liver, sometimes by excreting them unchanged through the kidneys. Two aspects of this process are important for the benzodiazepines.

First, the speed of onset of action depends on how the medicine is given and how quickly it gets into the brain. If a benzodiazepine like diazepam is injected into a vein, it is immediately in the blood stream and gets to the blood supply to the brain in less than 30 seconds, starting to have an effect within a few minutes. This rapid action is very useful in sedating a person for an operation or stopping an epileptic fit.

The usual way to take a medicine is to swallow a tablet or capsule of it. This then dissolves in the stomach and is absorbed from there and from the upper gut. It takes roughly 20–90 minutes for the medicine to get into the blood stream, from where it can pass across into the brain. Effects come on in 30 minutes, peak at about an hour and lessen over the next two to four hours. Some benzodiazepines, such as diazepam, are quite rapidly absorbed by mouth; others, such as oxazepam, less quickly.

Second, on absorption into the blood stream, the drug is circulated throughout all the tissues of the body, including the liver. Here it is broken down so that it can be eliminated from the body. In fact, the liver deals with drugs as if they were poisons or toxins. Thus, a competition ensues between the drug getting into the brain and hopefully having the beneficial effect intended, and being got rid of by the liver. Eventually, the entire dose of the drug is disposed of, and the effect ceases.

Some benzodiazepines are quite short-acting, others last much longer. Some are broken down into metabolites, which are themselves active, prolonging the effect, until they are in turn destroyed by the liver. Chlordiazepoxide and diazepam are long-acting because they are slowly broken down but also give rise to a very persistent active derivative. Lorazepam and oxazepam are medium in duration and have no active metabolites (see Table 7.1).

Table 7.1 Some benzodiazepine tranquillizers

Compound	Trade name	Half-life
alprazolam	Xanax (not available in the UK)	12–15 hours
chlordiazepoxide	none – used to be Librium	6–30 hours
diazepam	none – used to be Valium	1–4 days
lorazepam	none – used to be Ativan	12–16 hours
oxazepam	none – used to be Serenid	7–20 hours

The efficiency of the liver in dealing with medicines like the benzodiazepines varies greatly from individual to individual. In someone who is a rapid metabolizer, the effects will tend to wear off quickly. A slow metabolizer, by contrast, will experience prolonged effects of substances. Indeed, medicines may build up in the body because the liver cannot dispose of them rapidly enough. Children, the elderly and the physically ill also tend to break down medicines more slowly than healthy young adults.

How benzodiazepines work

This is a highly technical subject, involving the properties of special proteins on the surface of brain cells (neurons) that are called receptors. In essence, benzodiazepines bind to one particular type of receptor and dampen down activity in those cells. This is called 'inhibition'. Without normal inhibition in the brain we would all be in permanent panics, epileptic fits, muscle spasms or we would never sleep. Benzodiazepines increase the degree of normal inhibition in the brain so that we become less anxious, do not have fits, can relax and sleep.

The action of benzodiazepines can be blocked by a drug called flumazenil. This can reverse the effects of benzodiazepines – to counter the effects of an overdose, for example.

Several parts of the nervous system are affected by the benzodiazepines. The spinal cord is the site of action where muscle relaxation can be induced by lessening activity in the nerve cells there. Anticonvulsive effects may be caused by lessening activity in the lowest part of the brain, the brainstem. The cerebellum lies under the main part of the brain and co-ordinates movement. Interference with its activity by benzodiazepines causes lack of co-ordination, evidenced in staggering and disruption of eye movements. The 'limbic' areas of the brain are involved in emotional expression and control. The benzodiazepines can dampen down emotional feelings or, on occasion, do the opposite, releasing emotions excessively. Finally, the highest and by far the most extensive parts of the brain, the cerebral cortices, control all higher functions, such as judgement, attention and fine movement. These can be impaired by the use of benzodiazepines, particularly at higher doses.

Clinical uses

The benzodiazepines are widely prescribed by doctors. Studies trying to measure how beneficial they are to patients, and assess their side effects, total many tens of thousands. The main problems for which they are prescribed, the 'indications', are insomnia (see later this chapter) and the range of anxiety disorders described in Chapter 4. Some forms of epilepsy and muscle spasm are also accepted indications. However, quite often a benzodiazepine is prescribed without the diagnosis of a clearly defined disorder, rather just worry, anxiety or vague psychological problems. This has been common practice since the benzodiazepines were first introduced in the 1960s, and underlies many of the problems found in their use, in turn resulting in their falling into disrepute.

The benzodiazepines are widely used in general practice, in fact more so than by psychiatrists. Because of their perceived safety in overdose as compared with the barbiturates, they were dished out in vast quantities, without adequate care or follow-up. This was a major factor in the dependence and addiction problems that became apparent in the 1970s and thereafter. These problems became widely publicized, resulting in a reluctance to prescribe them on the part of many doctors, and a resistance to taking them by patients that was even more widespread. Curiously, this has resulted in a drop in prescriptions for anxiety disorders but not for sleeping difficulties.

The benzodiazepines are roughly equivalent in terms of effectiveness, and there is little to choose between them. Diazepam and lorazepam tended to be the most popular. Diazepam has a smoother, long-lasting action, whereas lorazepam is more suited for short-term or emergency use.

Because people vary in how sensitive they are to benzodiazepines, it is customary and indeed good practice to start with a low dosage, say diazepam 2 mg three times a day or lorazepam 0.5–1 mg twice a day. If the patient is comfortable on that dose, but still has symptoms, then cautious increases are usually made. The upper recommended doses are 10 mg three times a day for diazepam and 2 mg twice a day for lorazepam. These should only be exceeded under exceptional circumstances.

That is more easily said than done. The drawback of the benzodiazepines is that most people become used to the beneficial effects of these drugs – so-called 'tolerance'. Here, two effects tend to cancel each other out. First, tolerance occurs to the side effects, so the patient becomes more comfortable. But also, the beneficial effects wane, so that the patient has to keep increasing ('escalating') the dose in order to retain any benefit, such as calmness or induction of sleep. The topic of tolerance will be discussed further in Chapter 9, in the context of dependence and withdrawal.

Side effects

The unwanted effects of benzodiazepines are generally understandable as 'too much of a good thing'. Because the benzodiazepines reduce the activity of the brain in a fairly indiscriminate way, they do more than just lessen anxiety. Thus, they will lessen feelings of emotion, such as happiness, joy and pleasure. Patients often notice this but do not complain because they welcome the control of their fears. Other unpleasant emotions, such as anger, hostility, jealousy and depression, may be deadened as well. Other subjective effects are drowsiness and tiredness, dizziness and a feeling of bursting in the head. These are usually noticed after the first few doses, but usually lessen markedly after a week.

Patients may also feel that their motivation, attention and concentration are impaired. Testing by psychologists using standard tests of intelligence, memory and organizing ability clearly show deficits in performance – again, particularly in the first week or so. But tolerance may not occur with some brain functions such as memory. The worst scenario is that brain functions are objectively impaired but the patient feels normal. This presents obvious problems for skills such as driving, especially in the elderly.

'Paradoxical' responses can appear in some individuals, although it is not clear how frequent or serious these can be. Possibly one in 10 or one in 20 patients may be affected. The commonest event is an increase rather than a decrease in anxiety. A more dramatic reaction is an increase in hostile feelings, and these may culminate, in a few instances, in aggressive acts. Often the patient is puzzled by these feelings and may not associate them with having taken a benzodiazepine. The behaviour includes uncontrollable giggling, laughing or weeping, and acting out of character by shoplifting, sexual improprieties and unprovoked aggression.

The combination of a benzodiazepine and alcohol is particularly hazardous, and the person may not remember clearly what happened on such occasions. Sometimes, the person becomes depressed and may attempt suicide.

Benzodiazepines and anxiety disorders

Benzodiazepines are prescribed for people with any of the anxiety disorders, although proven benefit has been accepted in only a few indications. Higher doses are prescribed for patients with panic attacks than with unfocused anxiety. Benzodiazepines may be taken before a phobic individual enters his or her particular stress-inducing situation, such as going into a crowded supermarket or speaking in public. However, they are not usually particularly effective, and may even hamper performance or disinhibit the individual. Benzodiazepines are not usually given to treat obsessive-compulsive or post-traumatic stress disorders, except for secondary symptoms such as insomnia.

Benzodiazepines are not antidepressants, and indeed may seem to make depressed people worse because they lessen associated anxiety and make the depression more obvious.

Patients treated with benzodiazepines may appear to derive some symptomatic relief but it is usually less than total. Controlled clinical trials that show good benefits beyond three to four weeks of treatment are few and far between. The trap is that patients develop dependence, and when they try to cut down or stop, experience withdrawal symptoms, of which anxiety is an important constituent. This is misinterpreted as a return of the original anxiety, the benzodiazepine is reinstated and the merry-go-round starts, with the dire consequence of unnecessary and possibly harmful long-term use. Another benzodiazepine-dependent patient joins the ranks!

Overdose

Overdose with benzodiazepines is common because of their easy availability, but deaths are uncommon. Notwithstanding, the combination with alcohol is dangerous and has resulted in many fatalities. After an overdose, the patient sleeps for 24–48 hours and then wakes up. If the diagnosis is in doubt, the antidote drug, flumazenil, can be injected to try to cut short the coma.

Sleeping tablets

As emphasized earlier, barbiturates, benzodiazepines and similar drugs can act as both tranquillizers and sleeping tablets ('hypnotics'), depending on dosage and time of administration. Some barbiturates of medium duration were favoured as sleeping tablets, and the pattern has been repeated with the benzodiazepines.

The ideal properties of a hypnotic sleeping tablet are listed in Table 7.2. Unfortunately, no such medicine exists and the best we have are the newer compounds that are chemically not benzodiazepines but act in a very similar way. These are the so-called 'z-compounds' – zopiclone, zolpidem and zaleplon.

Sleeping tablets as a class divide into the long-, medium-, and short-acting (see Table 7.3). The long-acting medicines, like nitrazepam and flunitrazepam, have effects that persist right through the following day, and are largely unsuitable for use as sleep-inducers. Temazepam is the main medium-acting compound. It is reasonably effective but the effects persist into the day. It is also a drug regularly abused by addicts: it was formulated as a liquid and then as a gel, both of which could be injected, albeit with difficulty.

Table 7.2 Properties of an ideal sleeping tablet

1 It induces sleep without too much delay.
2 The insomniac stays asleep and does not wake earlier than he or she wants to.
3 The sleep is deep and not broken by frequent awakenings.
4 The person finds the sleep to be satisfying and wakes up refreshed.
5 There is no tired, 'hung-over' feeling the next day, particularly in the morning.
6 If the sleeping tablet is taken for several nights it continues to exert its beneficial effects.
7 There is no problem in stopping the medication.
8 If the person does wake in the night to go to the toilet, he or she is not dazed or unsteady.
9 There is no interaction with other medications or with alcohol.
10 There is no likelihood of becoming dependent or addicted.
11 The elderly are not unduly sensitive to the medication.
12 There are no serious unexpected side effects, such as loss of memory or depression.
13 The medication can be taken intermittently and not every night, without problem.
14 It is available in a liquid formulation, which can be measured out accurately.

Table 7.3 Some benzodiazepine sleeping tablets

Compound	Trade name	Half-life
flurazepam	Dalmane (not available in the UK)	1–4 days
loprazolam	none	12–16 hours
lormetazepam	none	8–12 hours
nitrazepam	Mogadon	18–24 hours
temazepam	none	7–11 hours
triazolam	(not available in the UK)	2–4 hours
zaleplon	Sonata	1–2 hours
zolpidem	Stilnoct	2–4 hours
zopiclone	Zimovane	4–8 hours
eszopiclone	(not available in the UK)	4–8 hours

Of the z-compounds, zopiclone is somewhat shorter-acting than temazepam, but effects can persist into the next day, especially in the elderly. Zolpidem has a duration of action of about four to six hours and does not usually give rise to sleepiness the next day. Zaleplon is the shortest-acting of all – indeed, its effects may wear off halfway through the night. A second tablet can then be taken without drowsiness on waking.

Side effects

These are the same as when benzodiazepines are taken to treat anxiety, but as taking a benzodiazepine or a z-compound to induce sleep takes place in the evening and the person should then go off to sleep, the effects of sedation are actually the required effect. Sedation is only a problem if the insomniac gets up in the night or if it persists the next morning. Thus, the main desired effect of a sleeping tablet and its chief unwanted effect are the same (sedation and sleepiness respectively), but separated in time by eight hours. Because medicines are broken down in us in the particular way described earlier in this chapter, any sleeping tablet that keeps the insomniac asleep throughout the night will inevitably still be working for part, at least, of the next day. Usage is therefore a trade-off: you can take a short-acting medicine to go to sleep, but perhaps wake early without hangover; or take a longer-acting drug, stay asleep but wake up feeling groggy.

Flunitrazepam has acquired the reputation of being very powerful. It is supposed to be slipped into a drink surreptitiously and to cause excessive sedation with loss of memory – the 'date-rape' drug. Very few cases have been authenticated by measuring blood levels in the victim. Rather, most cases can be attributed to the unwise use of alcohol.

Rebound, withdrawal and addiction in relation to tranquillizers and sleeping tablets will be dealt with in Chapter 11.

Other medications

Some other medicines are used to treat anxiety or insomnia but do not cause withdrawal problems. They are listed here.

- Buspirone for anxiety. This is slow in onset of action and not as effective as the benzodiazepines.
- Antihistamines, such as promethazine and hydroxyzine, can be used to lessen anxiety or induce sleep. They can produce excessive sedation.
- Beta-blockers have been used to treat some anxiety symptoms, such as palpitations. Unfortunately, they may induce nightmares.

Some other sedatives are associated with dependence – chloral and clomethiazole are examples.

Finally, antidepressants are used to treat a range of anxiety disorders. Some, such as amitriptyline, trazodone and mirtazapine, can be quite sedative and may be prescribed by some doctors to help sleep problems. Antidepressants in general are dealt with in the next chapter.

8

Antidepressants

Antidepressants were first introduced into medicine in the late 1950s. Before that, amphetamines were available but these are stimulants, not antidepressants. The difference is that amphetamines elevate mood and activity in everyone, whether depressed or not. People feel happier, often euphoric, and become sociable and disinhibited. Cocaine has similar effects. In higher doses amphetamines can cause anxiety, panics and severe insomnia. There is also a risk of addiction, in situations when the amphetamines are taken for social and not medical reasons. Another problem is that sustained high dosage can induce a form of paranoid psychosis very similar to schizophrenia. For all these reasons, amphetamines are rarely prescribed and will not be discussed further.

Monoamine oxidase inhibitors (MAOIs)

These were actually the first true antidepressants to be discovered – by accident, in the search for treatments for tuberculosis. They are listed in Table 8.1.

Table 8.1   Some monoamine oxidase inhibitors (MAOIs)

Drug	Trade name	Usual daily dosage range (mg)
phenelzine	Nardil	45–60
tranylcypromine	none – used to be Parnate	10–30
Reversible MAOI		
moclobemide	Manerix	300–600

Clinical effects

The MAOIs are traditionally used to treat the 'atypical' depressive disorders (see Chapter 6). They are particularly effective in lessening phobic anxiety.

Common side effects

One of these compounds, iproniazid, was found to lessen depressive symptoms in sufferers from tuberculosis. Several other compounds followed. They all blocked the activity of one of the enzymes that breaks down some brain chemical messengers, thereby increasing the activity of the brain mechanisms involved in the regulation of emotions. Unfortunately, the MAOI enzymes in the rest of the body were also inactivated, so that interactions with some other drugs and with some foodstuffs, such as cheese, became a serious problem (see Table 8.2). Despite being particularly useful in treating depressed patients with phobic symptoms, most MAOIs were withdrawn from use. One in particular, tranylcypromine, closely resembled amphetamines: it could be abused and cause overactivity. These medicines are largely obsolescent.

Table 8.2 Common side effects of MAOIs

- Drop in blood pressure
- Swelling of hands and feet
- Dangerous interactions with other drugs, e.g. nasal decongestants, and with foodstuffs, e.g. cheese

More selective MAOI medications have been developed, which include selegeline, also used in Parkinson's disease, and moclobemide.

Tricyclic antidepressants (TCAs)

The first of these, imipramine, was introduced soon after the MAOIs, but was much more successful. Chemically, it has three rings, so the group of antidepressants are called tricyclic. TCAs work by increasing brain chemical messengers, particularly serotonin and norepinephrine (also known as noradrenaline), but by a different mechanism than the MAOIs. Numerous medicines of this type have been marketed (see Table 8.3 on page 55).

One of the most widely used is amitriptyline; another, in the UK at least, is dosulepin (also known as dothiepin). Clomipramine is an interesting TCA in that it has powerful effects on serotonin, although its main metabolite primarily affects norepinephrine, thus losing the serotonin selectivity. Lofepramine resembles imipramine but has a better side effect profile and is safer in overdosage. Various other TCAs have their own pattern of effects.

Table 8.3 Some tricyclic and related antidepressants

Drug	Trade name	Usual daily dosage range (mg)
amitriptyline	none – used to be Tryptizol	50–200
clomipramine	Anafranil	20–150
dosulepin/dothiepin	Prothiaden	75–250
imipramine	none – used to be Tofranil	75–225
lofepramine	Lomont	70–210
nortriptyline	Allegron	75–150
trimipramine	Surmontil	50–150
Related compounds		
maprotiline	Ludiomil	50–150
mianserin	none	30–90
trazodone	Molipaxin	150–300

Clinical effects

The main indication for a TCA is major depression. However, other forms of depression, such as chronic mild symptoms, depressions in early dementia or schizophrenia, may also respond to some extent. The more pronounced the physical features in the depression, such as insomnia and lack of appetite and weight, the better the response to a TCA.

Roughly speaking, about two-thirds of really depressed individuals will respond to a TCA, although as many as a third will respond, at least temporarily, to dummy tablets (placebos). The symptoms that improve range from insomnia and lack of appetite to feelings of guilt and worthlessness. The core symptoms of depressed mood and lack of pleasure in life are particularly responsive. A delay of two to three weeks is generally expected before the patient feels any better, although the stirrings of improvement can be detected by a carer much earlier. Patients start to sleep better and wake refreshed and better able to face the world that day. They become more alert, able to attend and concentrate, and become more motivated to do things. Eventually, the patient states that she feels better, becomes optimistic and can see a future. Anxiety, either general or phobic, may be slower to lessen.

Common side effects

The question of suicide risk with all types of antidepressants has received publicity. Careful analyses of the facts show that the greatest risk in a depressive occurs in the month before – not after – treatment is started. However, as the patient becomes energetic before the mood lifts, he or she may be at risk as the medication starts to take effect. Careful supervision and close monitoring are required to prevent possible suicide events. Occasionally, antidepressants do appear to activate suicidal impulses, particularly in adolescents. As the effectiveness of antidepressants in children and adolescents has not been clearly established (except perhaps for fluoxetine), prescribing an antidepressant for these age groups should never be undertaken lightly.

The commonest side effects are listed in Table 8.4. The drowsiness and listlessness are akin to the effects of the older antihistamines. Sometimes the individual feels lightheaded and detached from reality. The sedation usually lessens after a week or two. Thinking, attention, concentration and memory may all be affected. As the patient is feeling slowed down because of the depression, when the medication is started, he or she will feel worse before starting to feel better.

Table 8.4   Common side effects of TCAs

- Dry mouth
- Constipation
- Blurring of vision
- Sedation
- Drop in blood pressure
- Weight gain

Dry mouth, blurring of vision and constipation are all caused by the same chemical effects. These can lead occasionally, particularly in the elderly, to mouth infections, paralysis of the bowel or confusion. Difficulty in urination may occur in males. A persistent fine trembling may be noted. Epileptic fits become more likely. Blood pressure tends to drop and the heart speeds up to try to compensate. TCAs also interfere with the working of the heart and may induce irregularities that can be hazardous or even lethal in overdose.

Sexual problems may be complained of, and include delayed ejaculation and orgasm, as well as loss of desire. A craving for carbohydrates may be noted, resulting in weight gain.

The most important drug interaction is with alcohol. The combination of a TCA and alcohol can result in excessive drowsiness and grossly impaired driving ability.

TCAs are highly dangerous in overdose and are one way of attempting suicide. Both breathing and heart function are impaired; the patient can sink into a coma, or develop fits, and may die.

A range of antidepressants that largely resemble the TCAs are available. They include:

- *mianserin*, which needs careful monitoring in the elderly because it can affect the white blood cells;
- *trazodone*, which is quite sedative and may be used to treat insomnia;
- *bupropion*, which is available as an aid to quit smoking but can also act as an antidepressant.

Selective serotonin re-uptake inhibitors (SSRIs)

The side effects of the TCAs are common, sometimes serious, but always troublesome, especially in the elderly. The drug company scientists knew that most of the side effects were avoidable since they resulted from actions that were not part of the antidepressants' properties. From the 1970s onwards, manufacturers tried to develop antidepressant medications that were much more selective than the rough-and-ready TCAs. This resulted in a series of selective serotonin re-uptake inhibitors that were marketed from the 1980s onwards.

The SSRIs are selective in two ways. First, they act on only one of the brain chemical messengers thought to be instrumental in depression, namely serotonin. Second, they do not affect bodily mechanisms that are incidental to the antidepressant response. Despite the claims of the drug makers, selectivity is not absolute. Fluoxetine, for example, has a breakdown product, norfluoxetine, that also acts on norepinephrine (noradrenaline); paroxetine can cause dry mouth and sedation, just like a TCA. Nevertheless, the SSRIs were regarded as a definite improvement over the TCAs in terms of side effects and safety, although no more effective in clinical practice.

The various SSRIs available today are listed in Table 8.5 (page 58). Another class of antidepressants (the SNRIs) is selective for two chemical messengers – serotonin and norepinephrine.

Clinical effectiveness

The SSRIs have been extensively studied, both in comparison with dummy medication, with the older TCAs and among themselves. The first studies involved patients with major depression, and the SSRIs are usually given a licence for this first. Next, clinical effects on a series of anxiety disorders are tested, usually with good benefit: various SSRIs are licensed in different types of anxiety. Some SSRIs are available for use in special indications – fluoxetine in bulimia, for example. Whatever the population of depressed and anxious patients tested, SSRIs usually have about equal effectiveness, although each drug manufacturer tries

Table 8.5   Some SSRIs and similar antidepressants

Drug	Trade name	Usual daily dosage range (mg)
SSRIs		
citalopram	Cipramil	20–60
escitalopram	Cipralex	10–20
fluoxetine	Prozac	20–60
fluvoxamine	Faverin	50–300
paroxetine	Seroxat	20–50
sertraline	Lustral	50–200
SNRIs		
duloxetine	Cymbalta	60
venlafaxine	Efexor	75–225
Other		
mirtazapine	Zispin	15–45
reboxetine	Edronax	4–12

to establish the superiority of their own product in at least one indication. Whether or not these claims stand up under scientific scrutiny does not concern us here.

What is important is how many patients show a worthwhile improvement when prescribed an SSRI. As with the TCAs, about two-thirds of depressed or anxious patients will respond, compared with a third given dummy medication. This still leaves a third who show little or no response – so-called 'refractory' patients. The strategies for trying to help these patients usually involve an increase in dose, a switch of medication or the addition of another form of treatment.

The onset of action is not prompt; rather, it comes on over days or weeks, which is why doctors will advise the patient to give the SSRI an adequate trial before giving up and trying an alternative. As with the TCAs, it is in this period that careful monitoring is essential – the patient should be seen frequently.

Side effects

The side effects of the SSRIs are usually less frequent and serious than with the TCAs (see Table 8.6). Patients can tolerate them better, and prefer them. The selectivity cannot take all the side effects away. Some, such as nausea and sexual problems, are actually caused by serotonin in the brain and in the body. Fortunately, they are usually related to dose, so lowering the dose may be all that is needed. Also, the side effects tend to lessen over time. For example, a patient may find the nausea

Table 8.6   Side effects of SSRIs

- Nausea
- Tremor
- Loss of appetite
- Insomnia
- Sexual problems
- Increase in anxiety early in treatment

after the first few doses quite upsetting, but finds it has disappeared by the end of the first week.

Paradoxically, the first week or so of treatment with an SSRI may increase anxiety rather than diminish it. Phobias and insomnia may also increase. To get round this in patients with anxiety disorders, the doctor should prescribe a half dose of the SSRI for the first week, and should alert the patient to the possible rise in anxiety symptoms.

Loss of appetite may follow the nausea, and may cause loss of weight. This is seen most often with fluoxetine. Diarrhoea can occur. Tremor has been noted in a few patients. Sexual side effects include failure to reach orgasm in women, and delayed ejaculation in men. Dissimilarly to the TCAs, the combination with alcohol does not usually result in increased intoxication.

One clear advantage of the SSRIs over the TCAs is their safety in overdose, accidental or deliberate. Effects on the breathing and the heart are minimal.

The debate still continues, 20 years after the introduction of the phenomenally successful SSRI, fluoxetine, as to whether the better tolerability and safety of such SSRIs justifies their price differential over the TCAs. This debate has become less fierce as one after another the SSRIs have lost their patent protection and cheap generic equivalents have become available.

The problems on stopping SSRIs are dealt with in Chapter 12.

Other drugs used as antidepressants

The drugs used to treat schizophrenia, the anti-psychotics, have been prescribed in low doses to depressed patients. Effects are not usually particularly impressive.

Benzodiazepines have been used to treat depressed patients. Sometimes this is because the doctor has missed an underlying depressive illness in a patient who comes complaining of anxiety, phobias or insomnia. Sometimes, the doctor is under the mistaken impression that benzodiazepines may help depression. All they do is lower the levels of anxiety, leaving the depressive symptoms unchanged.

Serotonin in the brain and body is made from an amino acid, a building block of protein. The particular precursor is L-tryptophan, and this given by mouth raises serotonin levels in the brain and may help some depressed patients.

9

What is withdrawal?

In this chapter I shall review the complicated area of withdrawal and dependence. There is controversy about the terms used and about their implications. Being warned that a drug is 'addicting' is much more worrying than being told it is 'only rebound'. But bear in mind that it is not important what names are used to describe symptoms that might occur when you try and stop medication. It is what you experience that counts. Rather than being sidetracked by disputes as to whether a medication is 'dependence-inducing' or 'addictive', you should ask your doctor these questions:

1   What is the likelihood of symptoms occurring on withdrawal?
2   How severe will they be?
3   When can I expect them to come on?
4   How long will they last?
5   Might they become distressing?
6   Will they interfere with my enjoyment of life?
7   Will they affect my social life, such as by preventing me from going out?
8   Will they lessen my efficiency at work or even prevent me working?
9   How I can avoid them?
10   If I cannot prevent them, can you treat them?
11   If you cannot treat them, what shall I do to cope with them?

Also ask any other questions that come to mind, and do all this before you accept any medication. Do not let your doctor fob you off with soothing statements.

The terms used

A confusing variety of terms and descriptions is used, some of which have different meanings in different contexts. The rest of this chapter discusses the commonest.

Discontinuation

This is the most neutral term used, and can refer to a symptom, syndrome or effect (see Chapter 3). It implies a clear sequence of stopping the medication that is then followed by typical symptoms and/or signs. This wording is preferred by pharmaceutical companies because it is neutral, in that no implication is made concerning dependence or addiction. Different syndromes with different causes, courses, symptom patterns, management and outlook can ensue:

Relapse

If the treatment has controlled symptoms of the illness by suppressing them rather than by correcting the underlying disorder, stopping that medication is very likely to be followed by a relapse as the symptoms of the disorder re-emerge. Anxiety symptoms can recur quite quickly, as can symptoms of poor sleep. With depressive illnesses, weeks or months may elapse before the patient recovers completely. With partial recovery, although the patient may no longer be really anxious or depressed, and tranquillity and optimism largely return, some symptoms, such as lack of appetite, may persist – and this usually means a higher risk of relapse if the drug is stopped.

Recurrence

Many illnesses are recurrent in that they occur in clearly separated episodes, with periods of normality in between. Depression is such a disorder. In the majority of sufferers from depression, particularly bipolar (manic-depressive) disorder, the patient is plagued by repeated illnesses, usually following a recognizable pattern. Drug discontinuation will not be followed by an immediate re-emergence of symptoms. A delay will occur, depending on the particular rhythm of the illness, although in some patients a pattern is difficult to discern. Some patients do not suffer another attack until assailed by stressful events, such as bereavement or redundancy; in others the cycle seems to be determined by biochemical tides in brain mechanisms.

Rebound

Most drugs act by binding to specialized protein molecules in the body called receptors. The drug locks on to the receptor that governs its action and either blocks it or activates it. This causes changes in the cell's activity. The body attempts to overcome these changes through compensating mechanisms that may involve further changes in the receptor numbers or characteristics, or in the cell upon which the receptor is sited. When the drug is stopped, it leaves the receptor, depending largely on the rate at which it is metabolized in the liver. As the concentration falls, the cell is left in its changed state. It then has to re-adapt back to its drug-free environment. Characteristic of rebound, therefore, is that its time-course is predictable from the rate at which the liver gets rid of the medication from the body.

Rebound occurs with many drugs. Thus, when a histamine-2 inhibitor, such as cimetidine (Tagamet), is used to treat gastric acidity, stopping it can be followed by a rebound increase in acidity and a return of indigestion. Inevitably, the patient fears that he or she has relapsed.

With agents acting on the brain, the best documented example is the use of sleeping tablets (hypnotic drugs). These drugs, such as temazepam, help induce sleep. Given repeatedly, the brain cells (neurons) try to overcome the reduction in activity induced by the drug. When the hypnotic is removed, the brain becomes overactive for a night or two, until the compensatory adaptive changes fade away. With antidepressants, one mechanism that has been put forward to explain discontinuation syndromes is that it is a rebound effect, not serious, and self-limiting, as the changes that the antidepressant has induced in the brain ebb away. We shall see that this is to underplay the whole problem.

Withdrawal

This has more implications than a simple, eventual return to the state before the medication was given. The cardinal feature of withdrawal is generally accepted to be the emergence of new symptoms, of which the patient has not previously complained. These are of a definable pattern, usually typical of each class of drug. They follow a predictable time-course, again mostly governed by the rate at which the medication disappears from the body. Thus, stopping heroin (diamorphine) is followed by different withdrawal symptoms from stopping a benzodiazepine. Stopping a long-acting benzodiazepine such as diazepam will produce withdrawal symptoms in days or even weeks; stopping a shorter-acting drug like lorazepam will be followed by symptoms, albeit similar to those after diazepam, but within 48 hours, and usually more intense. The duration of the withdrawal syndrome is somewhat less predictable, and persistent symptoms have been described. Withdrawal incorporates all the features of rebound, plus the definitive newly emergent discontinuation symptoms. A continuum between mild rebound and severe withdrawal therefore exists.

The likelihood and severity of withdrawal in a particular patient depends on a variety of influences, but many factors remain unclear. The best-understood include:

1 Higher doses usually increase the risk over lower doses.
2 Regular intake rather than sporadic use increases the risk of a withdrawal reaction.
3 The longer a drug is taken, the more stopping it is likely to be followed by withdrawal. It might also be that, if a patient finds it difficult to stop his medication because withdrawal symptoms appear every time he tries, then long-term usage will ensue.
4 Abrupt termination is more likely to lead to a severe withdrawal reaction than tapering. The explanation is that the compensatory changes following cessation have not had time to become fully effective. Tapering allows time for this to happen.
5 Some factors in the individual may be relevant, including gender, age, previous experience of the medication, use of multiple drugs, and possible biological factors, including genetically determined predisposition.
6 The best predictor is simply history. If the patient has had problems stopping that medication previously, it is more likely to happen again.

Tolerance

This can be defined as the reduced effect of the same dose of a medication on repeated administrations, which results in a need to increase the dose in order to maintain the same level of effect. In other words, the medication loses its effect over time. It is common with drugs of abuse, such as heroin and amphetamines. It used to be thought that tolerance had first to occur as seen by raising of the dose. Only then was discontinuation of medication followed by withdrawal. The example of the benzodiazepines shows this assumption to be wrong, as it is quite clear that patients maintained on moderate or even low doses may suffer a full withdrawal syndrome when they try to stop. That is also true of many antidepressants. **Habituation** is another term for tolerance, and implies that the effects wear off over time.

Dependence

This is shown by a compulsion to take a drug either to experience psychological effects or to avoid bodily or psychological discomfort in its absence. Therapeutically prescribed drugs, such as stimulants and sedatives, taken according to instructions, may cause both physical and psychological dependence. Psychotropic drugs are administered for their effects on the brain and emotions, so it may be difficult to decide whether continuing usage is to maintain a beneficial therapeutic effect or to stave off incipient withdrawal symptoms caused by an underlying state of dependence. This is the problem that most concerns both health professionals and the lay public, particularly patients taking psychotropic drugs. It may lead to a reluctance to take medication or to poor compliance with instructions on dosage and frequency.

Addiction

Addiction is a poorly defined term that primarily involves social factors. Other terms are drug misuse and drug abuse. The essential feature is that the 'addict' continues use of the drug despite physical dangers to herself, risk of occupational impairment and family and social problems. Drugs of addiction are classified in terms that are supposed to relate to the harmfulness attributed to the drug abuse, which often focuses on the actual or potential harm to society, not just the individual. Addiction to a particular drug may incorporate features of tolerance and physical and psychological dependence. Contrary to public misconceptions, many drug 'addicts' may be social or intermittent users. Only a minority become so 'hooked' that their lives revolve around activities, often illegal, necessary to guarantee a dependable supply of a drug. A drug may be deemed habit-forming when the individual makes a habit of its regular use; the term is usually restricted to drugs of misuse.

It must be emphasized that this whole area is controversial, with no firm consensus in many areas of the debate. Political considerations have also intruded on both domestic and international levels, and further blurred the issues.

10

Alternatives to medications

Introduction

Before tapering off a tranquillizer, a sleeping tablet or an antidepressant, it is essential that you have adopted other ways of coping with any anxiety, insomnia or depression respectively. It is no use giving up medication that might have been helping, at least a little, and leaving yourself without any other ways of dealing with the symptoms that might recur. It is understandable that someone who is sure that medications have not helped, or even made them worse, does not want to resort to medication again under any circumstances. But it is important not to be totally rigid and inflexible about this, as there are occasional exceptions. The commonest example is when someone with a definite depressive illness has been misdiagnosed as anxious and treated with a tranquillizer. This will not have helped the depression, only damped down the anxiety symptoms that masked the depression. The depression will resurface when the tranquillizer is stopped. In such an instance, agreeing to take one of the safer antidepressants may be wise, before the tranquillizer is withdrawn.

If an alternative medication is not indicated, as in most cases, learning to use non-drug methods of treatment is highly advisable before starting the withdrawal procedures. Otherwise, the person will be cast adrift without means of dealing with the anxiety or depression, should it come back. Often it is unclear to everybody whether the anxiety, insomnia or depression has resolved spontaneously (remitted), or whether it is being kept at bay by the continuing medication.

The non-medication therapies can be roughly divided into those that work and for which there is some rational basis, including counselling, psychotherapy, cognitive behavioural therapy and lifestyle changes, and those that work and for which no rational explanation can be found. Note the word 'rational'. There are always explanations to hand, but they may be unconvincing, improbable or violate the laws of physics and chemistry. In the latter group are acupuncture, raki, foot and cranial massage and so on, whatever new fad it is. Some people find therapies helpful, but this is a general 'placebo' effect. These procedures do improve symptoms in some people, but it has never been proven that this is a real therapeutic effect with a convincing explanation. But at least they are usually non-harmful – although sometimes the client's reliance on his guru assumes morbid intensity. But if you think it works, makes you less anxious and depressed and helps you sleep, then use it. The dangers are that you will spend a great deal of money on unproven remedies and may miss the opportunity to be given a proven method of treatment.

Homeopathy and herbal remedies are special cases. Homeopathy involves taking a highly diluted substance that is believed to induce the very symptoms that are being treated. There is no rational basis for this. The dilution is often so extreme that there are only a few molecules in a volume the size of the solar system. Again, it works by a placebo effect – homeopaths are skilled in taking a detailed history, including background and lifestyle, in contrast to the limited time a GP has available. Clients come to rely on homeopaths because of the therapeutic relationship established between them. The 'medication' is a sign of the continuing trust between them, but there is no real specific therapy involved, which also accounts for the lack of adverse effects. Numerous controlled studies have been carried out on homeopathic remedies, but the reality is that any apparent benefits can be put down to chance.

Herbal remedies, by contrast, do contain active chemical substances. The problem is that they often contain too many. It is difficult to standardize the extracts. Nevertheless, they can have definite therapeutic effects and, sometimes, adverse effects. Some of these have actually endangered life.

I shall review briefly the various active therapies with a rational basis. The others you can find from various sources, such as the internet, but I can endorse very few of them. Caveat emptor – buyer beware!

Counselling

This is a rather ill-defined form of therapy that can be offered to many people with the milder forms of anxiety, insomnia and depression. Counselling can be given by trained counsellors; many GPs have also acquired the necessary skills. There is a professional body for non-medical counsellors, who are often highly skilled and experienced. Try and find one of these to help you.

Often a single counselling session from the GP is sufficient to explain the causes and symptoms of the psychological disturbance, offer reassurance about eventual recovery and encouragement to deal with any particular problem. Especially early on, people are upset by their symptoms, find they interfere with daily activity, but in particular find them baffling, without obvious explanation. They feel alone in a terrifying internal world interacting with an even scarier environment, full of threats and ambiguities. Just to be told that they are not alone, that others suffer the same symptoms, and that it is even clearly recognized by the caring professions, can lift a heavy weight off a person. That is the first step in counselling.

The next is to provide the client with educational material. There is a lot available in doctors' surgeries and pharmacies. Those leaflets, pamphlets and books are usually reliable. As I said earlier, other sources, such as those on the internet, are less dependable – do not believe them uncritically.

Following the initial consultation with her GP, the client may be referred for counselling, often within the practice, by a full-time or part-time counsellor. Further interviews will take place over the ensuing weeks. The approaches can be roughly divided into directive (focal) and non-directive. The former probes a little into the client's earlier life, without being too intrusive. The counsellor should encourage the client to talk about adverse experiences, problems with parents and family, setbacks that still rankle. Uncovering these experiences is not an automatic guarantee that the emotional turmoil will be stilled. Rather, it gives the client the chance to air these conflicts, get them into the open and put them into perspective. Talking about them to a sympathetic individual who makes no judgements or criticisms can be very therapeutic.

The other form of counselling, non-directive, looks to the present and future, rather than to the past. Problems are dealt with as they arise and also as the fear of them arises. The client is advised about coping mechanisms. The 'here-and-now' advice may be very practical – for example, helping with financial problems by referral to the Citizens Advice Bureau. Counselling thus focuses on the interaction between the client and the environment, with some attention being paid to the particular fashion in which the client habitually responds to life events. Various outcomes and responses are considered. All along, clients should recognize the problems confronting them and should not expect to be given the solutions all laid out on a plate. Rather, a menu of options should be discussed.

The psychotherapies

These cover a range of techniques, from supportive psychotherapy (essentially non-directive counselling), individual psychodynamic psychotherapy and interpersonal therapy, to deep psychoanalytic psychotherapy and group therapies. They can be used to varying extents with sufferers from anxiety, insomnia and depression. Their essence is their reliance on various theories of the workings of the mind by such redoubtable figures as Freud, his daughter Anna Freud, Melanie Klein, Jung and Adler. There are innumerable theoretical considerations that operate within the mind, at both the conscious and unconscious levels; they are by their very nature difficult to evaluate scientifically. Even the effectiveness of the practice of psychotherapy is rarely put to the test. Evidence for effectiveness is scanty.

It is very difficult to be referred for psychotherapy within the NHS, and private treatment can involve a very expensive outlay. The more intensive analytic psychotherapies typically require four to five hours a week. Overall, it would not, therefore, be very useful to describe them in further detail here. Even if accessible, the psychotherapies (bar one) are not of particular relevance to withdrawal problems.

Group psychotherapy

The exception is group psychotherapy. This comprises usually six to eight people with psychological difficulties, who meet once a week for an hour to discuss those difficulties and to interact with each other. It needs a properly trained psychotherapist; otherwise the sessions can be a disaster, a few dominant individuals pontificating on the others' problems and the others withdrawing into their shells. This reflects the tendency of some people to confide in all and sundry, and for the rest to be naturally reluctant to air their personal difficulties, at least initially, to people they hardly know.

Most groups are made up of a variety of different clients with different problems, all mixed up together. But the groups can be more uniform, made up, for example, of those having problems with tranquilliser or antidepressant use. There are two approaches. The first is to wait until six to eight people with dependence problems have accumulated and to start them as a group, to help each other through withdrawal. The alternative, which I favour, is to have an ongoing group ranging from newcomers embarking on discontinuation through to those who have withdrawn successfully. It is the latter who give the former reassurance about what to expect, but also show that it can indeed be done. The group can go on indefinitely, but each member should be set realistic goals and not be allowed to continue indefinitely. Some people derive great support from the group, and even when free of medication, even of their symptoms, view with trepidation any suggestion that they should drop out to make room for beginners. The answer is for them to graduate to a post-withdrawal group, run by themselves, which is essentially a support team. It can be invaluable in preventing relapse.

Behaviour therapy

This is a somewhat outmoded therapy but still useful for specific phobias, such as of heights, flying and needles. Patients are first taught a relaxation technique. It does not much matter which – most are quite effective. They are then asked to imagine a 'hierarchy' of feared situations – for example, a spider (arachno) phobic might start with imagining a tiny money spider at the other end of the room, and end up with a great hairy tarantula on the back of her hand. Indeed, real-life (graded exposure) objects can be used. I have treated snake phobics with exposure to a friend's pet snake. The hierarchy is agreed with the therapist. Anxiety must be reduced at each stage before moving on to the next.

People with social phobia may combine gradual exposure to fearful social situations, such as public speaking, with assertiveness training and social-skill training. Other techniques are modelling and role-play, in which the client assumes various roles and rehearses responses to fear-inducing situations.

Agoraphobic people can be taught to introduce themselves gradually to the situations they fear. For example, they can start by imagining themselves going into a small friendly corner shop, then actually doing it, and then working up to a huge, noisy, crowded, impersonal hypermarket.

Obsessives can be taught how to stop themselves succumbing to their time-wasting rituals and thoughts by creating distracting routines. Various other techniques are available from the experts.

Cognitive behaviour therapy (CBT)

This has been the gold standard for psychological therapy in treating depression; it has been successfully transferred to treating the anxiety disorders; it is being adapted to manage various types of insomnia. The technique arises from an increasing awareness by psychologists that thoughts are important in influencing emotions and behaviour.

But not just any old thoughts! Negative thoughts are the culprit. You may regard the world as hostile or threatening, you may stay awake worrying or you may take a totally pessimistic view of things. A negative feedback is set up: negative thoughts produce anxiety and depression; these emotions colour the interpretation of the world, making it more anxiety- and depression-provoking and so on.

CBT aims to interrupt this vicious cycle at its most accessible point, namely at the thoughts. But this is not easy. A skilled, experienced therapist, usually a psychologist, is needed. And clients must commit themselves to attend regularly, and work hard, both within the sessions and in the real world.

In practice, you are likely to be asked to keep a diary. If you feel really anxious, sleepless or depressed, you jot down the time, the thought and how bad it made you feel. For example, you may meet a friend who is brusque with you, obviously trying to get away. It makes you feel depressed – 'She can't be bothered with me. Why? Because I *am* a useless, unattractive person.' The therapist will discuss this perception with you and offer alternative interpretations such as, 'She actually *was* late for an appointment. Didn't you say she was half-running before she noticed you?' In this way, more positive and less threatening interpretations can be substituted.

CBT not only helps anxiety, insomnia and depression, but can also prevent these conditions coming back again. That is because the person has learned more positive and constructive ways of thinking that she can put into practice every day. In fact, scientific studies have shown that in mild depression, CBT is better than antidepressant therapy; in moderate depression it is about equally effective; only in severe depression, with bodily features such as insomnia and weight loss, is it inferior.

CBT can be combined with medication, but studies of this are relatively few. We know little about how to combine the therapies, whether to give CBT first and then medications, or vice versa; or whether to give medication and then combine it with CBT as the person responds. These are all questions that are being worked out. It is not automatically a case of 'either/or'. Putting them together may be the most effective use of our scant NHS resources.

Relaxation techniques

There are many different types of relaxation technique, each with their gurus and disciples. It does not matter which you choose – find one that fits in with your lifestyle. It is the self-imposed discipline that is important. You may want to try a few, or even rotate them round from time to time.

Many of the techniques focus on mental relaxation, but some concentrate on muscular relaxation and bodily feelings. Respiratory control is often a part of the training.

Sleep hygiene

This rather curious term has been applied to a series of recommendations to improve sleep, most of which are just sound good sense (see Table 10.1).

First, the insomniac's complaints need evaluating, together with her or his expectations of a 'good night's sleep'. These complaints often become more frequent in middle and old age, and the belief has evolved that you need less sleep as you grow older. There is still some dispute over this, but it appears that many healthy older people sleep

Table 10.1 Sleep hygiene

Factor	Good hygiene
Environment	
Temperature	Avoid extremes
Noise	Avoid sporadic loud noises – install soundproofing
Sleep substances	Avoid caffeine, alcohol, nicotine
	Try a warm, milky drink
Sleep schedules	Keep to the same routine all week
	Limit daytime naps
Daily activities	Avoid excessive exercise
	Use moderate exercise later in the day
	Stop worrying in bed
	Have a good diet
Pre-sleep	Relax, have a warm bath
	Don't watch TV in bed

as well as they did as young adults. The problem is often physical complaints, such as aches and pains and coughing. The treatment should be symptomatic, directed towards these complaints.

The elderly do, however, spend more time in bed. They do not have to get to work, and for the impoverished, bed is often the warmest place in the house.

There are wide differences in sleep requirements and patterns. The physical environment, including the bed, is important. Some people like a hard bed, others a soft one. The temperature of the bedroom should avoid extremes of heat (75°F; 24°C) and cold (60°F; 15.5°C). Partners may interfere with each other's sleep, but the absence of the habitual loved one may also disrupt sleep. Gentle familiar noise or low music may be soothing and help sleep to come on, but loud sporadic noise can be very disruptive. Sensitivity to noise varies considerably, but anxious people and the elderly are generally more affected. Aircraft noise is a well-known problem as it is sporadic and can be quite loud.

Many substances can interfere with sleep and should be avoided or minimized. In some people alcohol taken as a 'nightcap' may disrupt sleep in the second half of the night. Coffee is the main concern. Even though many people assert that they can drink several cups of coffee or tea late at night with impunity, studies suggest that sleep can be affected adversely. Painkillers often contain caffeine, so the person may unwittingly take more than expected.

Psychological measures revolve around establishing firm behavioural routines. It is important to maintain a regular pattern of sleep, going to bed and getting up at the same time each day, including the weekends. Sleeping late at weekends delays the onset of sleep the next night, resulting in tiredness on Monday mornings. Napping during the day may suit some people but not others. If napping does occur, less sleep is needed that night.

Bedtime routines are important in establishing the day–night rhythms of life. Just think how much of a ritual going to bed is. This helps induce sleep as a sort of conditioned reflex. Children love these routines, such as a bedtime story and the statutory goodnight kiss!

Perhaps the most effective way to improve sleep is to take regular, moderate exercise. This is beneficial for general health as well. The late afternoon or early evening is the best time. Irregular, sporadic exercise, particularly if very vigorous, is unhelpful. Regular meals are important, and some people swear by their night-time milky drink. It is not advisable to have a heavy meal or drink too much fluid before retiring.

Good sleep hygiene advice may be sufficient to improve sleep without resorting to sleeping tablets. There are some psychological treatments that are effective, but they are not readily available yet and so will be described only briefly.

Psychological treatments for insomnia

Progressive muscular relaxation is commonly used. The client is taught to contract and relax groups of muscles in turn, starting with curling up the toes. Autogenic training is a mental exercise in which the subject repeats self-suggestions of warmth, heaviness and drowsiness.

Sleep is a complex state, combining bodily 24-hour sleep–wake cycles with conditioned routines. Stimulus control treatment aims to reinforce these rhythms. The subject only goes to bed when drowsy, and gets up again if sleep is delayed. If worry keeps the person awake, a period during the day is set aside to do this type of worrying. Sleep restriction is another technique in which clients are instructed to limit the time spent in bed, whether asleep or not.

CBT has various specialist techniques that seem effective but are only slowly becoming available.

Psychological treatments for depression

For mild depression, simple supportive therapy or more focused approaches such as marital therapy may suffice. Some psychotherapy may also be enough. Other techniques include lifestyle advice, increase of activities and problem-solving.

Cognitive behavioural therapy

This was described earlier and has been most widely applied to treat depressed people. The cognitive idea is that experience leads people to form beliefs about themselves, the world and the future. Critical incidents may lead to crucial interpretations that focus on the negative aspects. These negative thoughts and perceptions are first corrected and then transformed into positive beliefs. However, CBT requires skilled therapists and they are in short supply. Severe depression needs careful assessment lest CBT prove ineffective when the illness has progressed so far.

Interpersonal therapy

This was developed in the USA and is based on the assumption that the root cause of depression lies in an interpersonal context. Treatment focuses on enhancing the quality of current functioning between the client and people around her, particularly family and friends. It has been shown to be about as effective as antidepressants in milder depressives, and can be used to maintain remission. Like other psychological treatments, it is not widely available.

Conclusions

The non-medications form a long list. Some are known to be effective, such as CBT and relaxation. Others are much more dubious, still others totally devoid of either theoretical rationale or evidence of practical effectiveness. The danger is that by resorting to untried techniques, the depressive will be deprived of proven remedies.

11

Withdrawal from tranquillizers and sleeping tablets

This is still a somewhat controversial topic, although most debate about it took place in the 1980s. But the topic had its roots much further back than that. It was realized soon after the barbiturates were introduced at the start of the twentieth century that some people became accustomed to them; some increased the dosage at least tenfold; some abused them together with alcohol; many people found great difficulty in trying to stop the medication, and complained of severe symptoms on trying to do so. It was clear that these were both dependence-inducing and addictive drugs. That means that they caused the bodily makeup of users to change so that their metabolism was 'hooked' on barbiturates; and users would become further addicted taking high doses and endangering their physical and mental health, and their social and occupational performance.

When the benzodiazepines came in they were welcomed as much safer substitutes. This was because it seemed that they were much less likely than the barbiturates to kill people in high dose, such as overdose. This difference spilled over into the area of dependence because very few people increased the dose above the therapeutic range. But from the start, it was known that very high doses could induce a severe state of dependence. An experiment was carried out on American prisoners in gaol, in which the dose of the first benzodiazepine, chlordiazepoxide (Librium), was pushed up and up at least tenfold. When the Librium was stopped, all of the unfortunate men developed severe withdrawal reactions and some had epileptic fits. Such a study would not get past an ethical committee nowadays.

As time went by, this study came to be regarded as an aberration. As Librium and then Valium became widely prescribed, it appeared that very few people taking them increased the dose. This had previously been taken as an essential sign that dependence was developing. The prescribers and the public were lulled into a false sense of security that benzodiazepines, as well as being much safer in overdosage than the barbiturates, were almost free of dependence or addiction liability. Sales steadily rose until, worldwide, Valium was the most successful drug ever.

Not only did more and more people take a benzodiazepine, but more and more people stayed on them. Because they had stayed on the same dose from the start, it was assumed there was no problem. Medical and scientific investigators began to ask the question, 'If the benzodiazepines do not induce dependence, why are so many people taking them for so long?' My research team was the first to investigate this puzzle in an organized way. Soon, it became clear that even people taking therapeutic doses, say 10–15 mg diazepam, developed full-blown reactions if they tried to stop. This was so even if they tried to taper off diazepam, which is anyway a long-acting compound that 'self-tapers'. They were physically and psychologically dependent. Other teams also came to the same conclusion (Ashton; Tyrer) and the concept of normal-dose dependence emerged.

The media seized on this as yet another example of the irresponsibility of the prescribing doctors, and particularly of the manufacturers of tranquillizers such as diazepam (Roche) and lorazepam (Wyeth). Numerous television and radio programmes were produced, all highlighting the dangers of longer-term use (say a month or more) of the benzodiazepines.

There were dissident voices. Some doctors refused to acknowledge that tolerance and increase in dose were not necessary for the development of dependence. The drug manufacturers denied that their products were defective, and blamed the problem on the 'addictive personalities' of the dependent subjects. Concern varied from country to country, the UK taking the matter very seriously, France and Germany less so. Prescriptions for tranquillizers fell, while those for sleeping tablets stayed buoyant.

Some studies suggested that, like alcohol, benzodiazepines taken long term could be associated with brain damage and shrinkage that was only reversible when the person finally managed to stop. This has never been clearly confirmed, and people should not worry too much about the possibility.

Attempts to help people dependent on benzodiazepines took many forms. Setting up support groups was probably the most useful. Giving out educational material was also popular, but some of the leaflets were unduly alarmist.

Currently, benzodiazepines are still widely used as tranquillizers or sleeping pills. Each class of medication is prescribed at about the same rate, but there has been a drop of about a third in the prescription of sleeping tablets over the last ten years, yet no change in the rate of prescription of tranquillizers. By far the most frequently prescribed tranquillizer is diazepam (old trade name Valium). Temazepam was widely used as a sleeping tablet but its usage has declined markedly. A similar compound, zopiclone, is now the most popular sleeping tablet.

How frequent is the withdrawal syndrome?

The syndrome needs to be defined. I proposed many years ago that a withdrawal syndrome may follow the stopping of medication, with a characteristic time interval mainly dependent on the half-life of the compound. The syndrome comprises at least four signs and symptoms that were not present before discontinuation or even before treatment – 'discontinuation-emergent symptoms'. It should tend to follow a typical time-course and disappears in most cases. It is more likely to occur if the medication is stopped abruptly. Re-prescribing the compound, or one in the same class, usually but not always results in rapid disappearance of the symptoms.

Bearing this definition in mind, several studies have looked at the incidence of withdrawal reactions from benzodiazepines and similar compounds. At high doses, beyond the usual therapeutic range, a withdrawal reaction is almost inevitable unless very slow tapering is carried out. At therapeutic doses, about one in three individuals will report reactions, even with tapering. One in three of these are clinically important in that the sufferer seeks advice of some sort from his or her GP or a support group. Among this ten per cent of the original users, a third will have severe or protracted symptoms. To repeat – one in ten will have definite problems; one in thirty is really badly affected.

However, these figures were derived many years ago, in the 1980s. Our techniques have been refined since then, but few further studies have been organized, carried out and completed. By and large, the responsible manufacturers have not put resources into thoroughly investigating this entire problem. One senses that they are still trying to brush the problem under the carpet.

There are obvious differences among the benzodiazepines. Chlordiazepoxide (Librium) and diazepam (Valium) have low rates of withdrawal problems. A general consensus has arisen that lorazepam (Ativan) poses more problems than any of the others in its class. This probably reflects its short half-life (12 hours on average) as compared with over 100 hours for Librium and Valium, and their active metabolites. Oxazepam has a similar half-life to lorazepam but gives fewer problems, which means factors other than half-life must be operating. This gets to be very technical.

Symptoms of withdrawal from benzodiazepine tranquillizers and clinical course

Over 25 years ago, together with my colleague from Iceland, Professor Hannes Petursson, I carried out a placebo-controlled study in 22 patients who were tapering off their benzodiazepine. The design of the study was quite elaborate in order that we could be sure that any symptoms reported were really due to the withdrawal and not chance events or fanciful elaborations of normal feelings in the mind or body. We carried out a whole series of psychological tests and measured blood levels of benzodiazepines over eight weeks. Finally, the patients were seen again at a 12-week follow-up appointment.

The numbers of patients experiencing various symptoms at 0–2 weeks, 2–4 weeks and at follow-up are shown in Table 11.1.

Table 11.1 Numbers of patients out of 22 experiencing withdrawal symptoms, up to two, between two and four weeks, and at follow-up

Symptoms	0–2 weeks	2–4 weeks	Follow-up
Anxiety, tension	22	11	5
Agitation, restlessness	9	5	0
Irritability	9	2	0
Lack of energy	7	0	1
Impaired memory and concentration	7	1	0
Depression	5	7	1
Feelings of unreality	5	1	0
Sleep disturbance	20	7	2
Loss of appetite	15	3	0
Headache	12	2	0
Muscle pains, aches, twitching	11	2	1
Nausea, dry retching	10	1	1
Tremor, shakiness	10	1	0
Perspiration	9	1	0
Other bodily symptoms	8	1	0
Metallic taste, oversensitive smell	14	2	0
Pins and needles	14	4	0
Sore eyes, photophobia	13	5	0
Lack of coordination, vertigo	11	4	0
Oversensitive hearing	9	2	0
Flu-like illness	9	0	1
Oversensitivity to touch and pain	4	1	0
Paranoid reaction	3	1	0
Visual hallucinations	1	0	0

The most frequent symptoms between one and two weeks after stopping were anxiety and tension, followed by sleep disturbance and loss of appetite (accompanied by loss of weight). Symptoms of perceptual disturbance included a metallic taste in the mouth and peculiar smells. Patients complained of sore eyes and of lights appearing bright. Headache, muscle pains, aches and twitches were complained of by half the patients, as were unsteadiness and dizziness, nausea and trembling. Some patients felt just physically ill and weak all the time, as if they had contracted influenza.

Between two and four weeks after stopping, these symptoms were present in less than half the patients, and some had almost disappeared. At follow-up at 12 weeks, some symptoms still lingered on – anxiety, tension and insomnia.

During withdrawal, the symptoms could be very severe. Some anxious patients began to suffer from panics; many became unusually irritable. Some even became depressed for a while, and this persisted in one patient. The most serious reactions were seen in three patients who lost contact with reality for a few days. Paranoid reactions were seen in three patients and one saw faces and patterns on a wall. All these reactions subsided with specific anti-psychotic medication.

Appetite loss could be severe, and the patients lost an average of about 1–1.5 kilos in weight. A range of physiological measures, such as EEG (brainwaves), showed temporary disruption. Psychological performance, such as reaction time, was also below par. By contrast, some measures of biochemical brain function increased, suggesting stress.

High dose versus low dose – tapering versus abrupt discontinuation

Another study that my team carried out (lead worker Dr Cosmo Hallstrom) showed, somewhat to our surprise, that the intensity of the withdrawal reaction was the same in people coming off high doses above the therapeutic range and those who had stayed within that range. All these patients tapered their doses. High doses should never be stopped abruptly, even with long-acting drugs such as diazepam. The danger is the onset of epileptic fits, which can be persistent and difficult to treat. Another problem is a psychotic reaction – loss of contact with reality, including paranoid reactions. We have already seen that tapering can lessen both the incidence and severity of withdrawal reactions but cannot prevent them entirely. Otherwise, there would be no problems coming off diazepam.

Implications for the user

Coming off tranquillizers can be a minor problem for about a third of users and a major ordeal for a small percentage. It is not surprising that many anxious people are reluctant to embark on a course of tranquillizers – they fear becoming dependent or addicted. The first is a realistic fear, as we have seen earlier. The upshot is that the anxious person keeps on taking the medication at the same dose indefinitely when he does not really need it – the tranquillizer is preventing the onset of withdrawal symptoms rather than lessening true anxiety. The second fear, addiction, would result in the person losing control of their tranquillizer use, pushing up the dose, taking alarming amounts in a chaotic fashion and perhaps combining them with unwise amounts of alcohol. This scenario is not common, and there is often a prior history of problems with tranquillizers and alcohol. Some drug addicts abuse the benzodiazepines, as part of multiple drug abuse – heroin, cocaine, amphetamines – but they are a totally separate group.

Over the past ten years, one development has been the increasing use of SSRI antidepressants to manage anxiety disorders. For the first time, doctors and patients have an alternative to the dependence-inducing benzodiazepines. Although, as we shall see in the next chapter, the SSRIs also have withdrawal problems, the treatment advantages generally outweigh these. Therefore, the situation has changed. If doctor and patient decide that the anxiety is severe enough to need medication, they now have a choice, balancing the immediate effects of benzodiazepines with the risk of dependence, against the slower effects of the SSRIs with some possible problems on trying to stop. I would usually use an SSRI, but select one with a low incidence of withdrawal problems.

A brief history of a long story

A description of a woman's dependence on tranquillizers:

> Helen is aged 45, married with three children. She was first placed on tranquillizers when she was 18, following a spontaneous miscarriage. For many years she has taken diazepam 5 mg, three times a day. On four occasions she has tried to taper off the medication but without much support. Whenever she tries, she becomes very anxious and finds it difficult to sleep. In particular, she notes that noises become very loud and lights impossibly bright.
>
> Her GP retired and the new one was very concerned about her long-term intake of tranquillizers. He put her in touch with a group that was being run by a woman who had gone through the same problems of

dependence. Helen joined. She was first taught some relaxation therapy and how to cope with any anxiety that might occur. She was then very carefully, over nine months, tapered off her 15 mg a day diazepam. She did develop some symptoms, such as feelings of not 'being with it', and severe muscle tension in her back, but with support she could cope with these, and the symptoms gradually lessened.

At present she remains off the tranquillizers, although at times she still feels tempted to go back on them. She has now gone on to a follow-up group that gives her support, and her husband attends with her. It is probable that she will be able to manage without relapsing into her dependent state.

Withdrawal from sleeping tablets

Earlier we saw that sleeping tablets range from long-acting compounds, such as nitrazepam (Mogadon), through medium-acting medicines like temazepam, to the short-acting zopiclone, zolpidem and zaleplon. The long- and medium-acting compounds persist during the day and thus act like tranquillizers. Withdrawal from these medications is the same as that from tranquillizers like diazepam and lorazepam, which I have dealt with earlier in this chapter.

With the short-acting compounds, the question is whether problems can actually arise with a medication that is cleared from the body within 24 hours. In other words, by the time the next sleeping tablet is due, say at 11 p.m., the body is free of the previous night's dose. People vary with respect to how quickly they get rid of a medication. With zopiclone, quite a few will have this in their bodies all 24 hours; with zolpidem, the number drops markedly; with zaleplon, almost everybody will metabolize it completely within 24 hours.

As a consequence, some people can develop dependence on zopiclone, a few on zolpidem, but probably nobody on zaleplon. Withdrawal might therefore be a problem in only a few people. Instead, because of the short duration of action of these three 'z-drugs', rebound may be disturbing. For a night or two after stopping the medication, sleep is slow in onset and can be broken with dreams or nightmares. The rebound usually lasts for only a night or so, so ex-users should not panic and resume their medication.

Conclusion

It is now generally accepted that a proportion of people who have taken tranquillizers for a long time will develop symptoms on trying to stop. In about one in ten such users, this is a real clinical problem. One in 30 has very major difficulties and will need expert help to withdraw successfully. The usefulness of these medications should continue to be debated, especially as alternatives are increasingly available.

12

Withdrawal from antidepressants

All of the antidepressants can give rise to discontinuation problems to a greater or lesser extent. However, in view of the widespread and increasing use of the SSRI and SNRI classes of antidepressant (see Chapter 8), I shall concentrate on these. But first I shall deal with the older compounds, the tricyclics (TCAs) and the monoamine oxidase inhibitors (MAOIs), which were also discussed in Chapter 8.

Withdrawal from TCAs

Imipramine was made available for prescription use in Switzerland in 1957 and in many other countries by the end of that decade. Very soon reports of problems encountered by patients who tried to stop imipramine began to appear in the scientific literature. As each new TCA was marketed, reports were soon published of some patients not being able to stop without incident. In the UK, by the 1980s Peter Tyrer, a psychiatrist with a special interest in withdrawal problems, had provided comprehensive accounts of these problems. He found them to be more likely after long-term use, high doses and abrupt discontinuation.

The symptoms reported fall into four groupings (see Table 12.1). The symptoms usually come on within a few days of stopping the TCA and are generally mild. Some of the symptoms, such as diarrhoea, reflect

Table 12.1 Withdrawal symptoms from TCAs

Group 1	General bodily symptoms
	Tiredness, headache, trembling, sweating and loss of appetite
Group 2	Emotional symptoms
	Anxiety and agitation, feeling miserable and tearful, irritability
Group 3	Sleep disturbance
	Broken sleep, problems falling asleep, nightmares and excessive dreaming
Group 4	Symptoms of the digestive system
	Nausea, retching, vomiting, loose bowels and diarrhoea

rebound in one of the chemical neurotransmitter systems, involving the chemical messenger acetylcholine. Even with treatment, the symptoms are short-lived, rarely lasting beyond a few days or a week. If the emotional symptoms persist, the person may be experiencing a relapse rather than a withdrawal.

Withdrawal from MAOIs

These drugs are used much less frequently than TCAs or SSRIs but may give disproportionate difficulties. Tranylcypromine is an amphetamine-like compound and can cause an amphetamine-type addiction. The MAOIs in general may result in a severe syndrome on withdrawal – confusion, paranoid ideas and hallucinations. The commonest symptoms are anxiety and agitation, a feeling of unreality and sounds seeming overwhelmingly loud. Rebound with a worsening of depression can be very noticeable.

Withdrawal from SSRIs

This has been the main focus of attention since the early 1990s, with the introduction of paroxetine (Seroxat). But all the other SSRIs have been implicated to a greater or lesser extent, and it is worth going into a little more detail.

The first consideration is to define the syndrome. Criteria for the SSRI withdrawal syndrome were set up in 1996 at a conference held in Phoenix, Arizona (see Table 12.2). These criteria were based on those earlier suggested by me with respect to tranquillizers.

Table 12.2 Criteria for SSRI withdrawal

1 Symptoms of the SSRI discontinuation or withdrawal syndrome should not be attributable to other causes.
2 The symptoms emerge after medication is discontinued abruptly, following a period of non-compliance with missed or forgotten doses, or following dose reduction.
3 The symptoms are usually transient and mild, but at times can become serious.
4 The symptoms are generally short-lived, mostly disappearing within two weeks, but can occasionally persist for several weeks.
5 If the original or a pharmacologically similar antidepressant is reintroduced, the symptoms remit, usually within 24 hours.
6 The syndrome can be minimized by tapering the shorter-acting SSRIs extremely slowly or by selecting a drug with an extended half-life, such as fluoxetine.

How frequent is the syndrome?

There are various ways of attempting to estimate the likelihood of symptoms troubling the person when she tries to stop. First, doctors write letters to medical journals to alert their colleagues to the possibility of symptoms. There follows a spate of reports, which then lessen: it is no longer newsworthy, as the medical profession moves on to the next crisis-of-the-moment. Patients and carers may contact helplines for advice about symptoms that have arisen following attempted withdrawal. The Maudsley, a hospital for mental illness in Camberwell, South London, runs such a helpline. Between October 1997 and March 2005, about eight in 100 calls referred to discontinuation from SSRIs. About 40 per cent involved paroxetine and 20 per cent venlafaxine. The paroxetine-related calls shot up following a *Panorama* TV programme on the drug.

The next source of data is the adverse reaction databases held by such agencies as the Committee on Safety of Medicines (CSM). Doctors and pharmacists in the UK report cases to a register held by the CSM. Again, in the 1990s the reporting rate for paroxetine was higher than for the other SSRIs available at that time, after taking the number of prescriptions into account. This type of data can also be obtained by asking GPs to report any unexpected reactions in their patients' prescribed medications (prescription event monitoring, PEM). In such a study rates were actually low, but this anomaly can be explained by GPs not recognizing the syndrome, particularly in its milder forms.

Another strategy is to take patients on various medications and substitute dummy tablets for a few days (interruption studies). Specific symptoms are rated. Such studies are usually now carried out routinely when a drug manufacturer is testing out a new drug before applying for approval for marketing. Another strategy is to study patients stopping their medication at the end of their period of treatment by switching them, either abruptly or gradually, to dummy medication. SSRIs vary greatly in the likelihood of symptoms developing at that time.

Scientific problems prevent the ready interpretation of some of these studies. I have mentioned that many doctors are hazy about the existence of withdrawal symptoms, and so may overlook them. If the withdrawal is delayed for a few days, as may happen with fluoxetine, then interrupting treatment for only a few days is not going to detect withdrawal problems. But all in all, paroxetine appears to have the highest incidence of withdrawal problems of any SSRI. On abrupt withdrawal, about one in three patients taking the medication will experience troublesome symptoms; but even if they taper it off, one in six will still be upset by symptoms. (I will return to tapering versus non-tapering a little later.) The order after paroxetine is fluvoxamine, sertraline, citalopram and escitalopram, with fluoxetine bringing up the rear. Why is this? The most likely explanation relates to the length of action of the various SSRIs. We have seen that this is dependent on the half-life of the medication (see Chapter 9). The faster the medication moves off the receptors in the brain, the more likely is a reaction and the more severe it is likely to be. Paroxetine has a relatively short half-life (10–21 hours) in the whole population. Fluvoxamine's half-life is a little longer, at 15–22 hours. Sertraline's is around 26 hours, but it is broken down in the liver to norsertraline, which has similar effects but with a much longer half-life (66–104 hours). The longest of all is fluoxetine, at 48–72 hours; it also has an active metabolite with a half-life up to 300 hours. It takes about four half-lives for the drug to clear from the body and brain, meaning from a day and a half to up to three and a half days for paroxetine, as contrasted with as long as several weeks for the active metabolite of fluoxetine. Withdrawal reactions are at a low incidence and delayed with fluoxetine, a possible major advantage commercially over paroxetine. It is hardly surprising that the makers of fluoxetine (Prozac), Eli Lilly and Company, sponsored many of the studies that compared the various SSRIs.

Symptoms of SSRI withdrawal

Two studies looked in detail at the symptoms following SSRI withdrawal. Dr Peter Haddad of Manchester University carried out a study in the UK; Dr Kathy Black and her Canadian colleagues reviewed the scientific literature from around the world. Their suggested criteria are listed in Table 12.3 (page 88). It can be seen that there is substantial agreement.

Another way of looking at this is to group the symptoms as in Table 12.1 (see page 84) for the TCAs and to add two or three new groups. The first is problems with balance, such as dizziness, vertigo and unsteadiness. The second is abnormalities of sensation, such as numbness, pins and needles in arms and legs and electric-shock-like sensations. The last are particularly upsetting: they often start in the head and run down the whole of the body, and can be felt several times a day.

Clinical course

Most patients who experience withdrawal symptoms do so within one to three days of stopping their medication. Symptoms can occur on reducing rather than stopping the medication. Occasionally, especially with fluoxetine, days or weeks may elapse before some symptoms come on that appear to resemble symptoms noted with other SSRIs.

Table 12.3   Criteria for withdrawal symptoms from SSRIs

- Symptoms follow discontinuation of, or reduction in dose of, an SSRI after at least one month of use.
- Two or more of the following symptoms appear within one to seven or ten days of discontinuation.
- The symptoms cause significant distress or impairment.

Haddad	Black and others
1 Dizziness or light-headedness	1 Dizziness, light-headedness,
2 Nausea or vomiting	vertigo or feeling faint
3 Headache	2 Nausea and/or vomiting
4 Lethargy	3 Headache
5 Anxiety or agitation	4 Visual disturbances
6 Tingling, numbness or	5 Anxiety
electric-shock sensations	6 Shock-like sensations or tingling
7 Tremor	7 Tremor
8 Sweating	8 Fatigue
9 Insomnia	9 Insomnia
10 Irritability	10 Irritability
11 Vertigo	11 Gait instability
12 Diarrhoea	12 Diarrhoea

Even without treatment, most patients find that their symptoms are mild. A small proportion, nonetheless, experience severe and alarming symptoms, and are particularly upset by the nausea, unsteadiness and the electric shock symptoms. Indeed, the Food and Drug Administration (FDA) in the USA warned some years ago that the withdrawal reaction could be severe.

Most symptoms disappear within a week but occasionally can be protracted. Some symptoms appear to last for months, a problem similar to protracted withdrawal reactions from tranquillizers.

The likelihood of getting withdrawal problems does not seem to be related to age or gender. The dosage level has some influence, as has duration of treatment. The important thing to note is that withdrawal can follow quite low doses of SSRIs given for a few weeks. In other words, it can follow quite standard courses of treatment for a depressive or anxiety disorder. A factor that showed up in one study is that people who get adverse effects when they start treatment are more likely to get adverse effects when they try to stop. This might just reflect the possibility that they are on higher doses.

Tapering versus abrupt discontinuation

The question as to whether reducing the dose gradually (tapering) can prevent withdrawal reactions is crucial in establishing whether following the procedures recommended by the official Data Sheets is sufficient. If it is not, then more elaborate procedures will need to be followed. Even these may not prevent the reaction totally or reduce it to bearable levels. Unfortunately, the evidence is not thick on the ground. Recommendations were made almost from the introduction of the various SSRIs. Indeed, paroxetine (Seroxat) was marketed in 1990 with the following suggestion: 'As with any psychoactive medicine it may be prudent to discontinue therapy gradually because of the possibility of discontinuation symptoms such as disturbed sleep, irritability and dizziness.'

Reports of withdrawal reactions still occurred, but many related to stopping abruptly, and often quite high doses. A Japanese study suggested that about two-thirds of people will get significant symptoms if they stop suddenly, as compared with one in five who gradually withdraw. A study in the Netherlands noted that twice as many withdrawal symptoms occurred in those who stopped their SSRI abruptly, compared with those who tapered off their medication. Other studies suggest that tapering does not always work: other strategies are needed as well.

Implications for the user

Does it matter? The symptoms are usually mild and go away by themselves. But we have seen that sometimes the symptoms can be severe and upsetting. The FDA warned about this some time ago. Some of the symptoms, such as the shock-like sensations, can be very alarming and lead the person to fear that he is suffering from a neurological condition, such as multiple sclerosis. If the prescribing doctor is unaware of SSRI withdrawal, the person may be sent to hospital for unnecessary and unpleasant investigations; or it is assumed that relapse is occurring and the antidepressant is started again unnecessarily.

Because SSRIs have been heavily promoted by their manufacturers, any adverse effects of this type tend to be played down. When they are made public through the professional and lay media, the public lose confidence, not only in the individual medication but with antidepressants in general. This spills over into the prescribers – GPs and psychiatrists. The loss of confidence can lead depressed people to refuse to take medication because they regard it as 'addictive'; and if they do have the medication dispensed at the pharmacist, they take it in a desultory fashion.

The detailed advice now provided in the official Data Sheet for Seroxat is set out in the Appendix.

Withdrawal from SNRIs

The two main compounds here are venlafaxine and duloxetine. Venlafaxine lies between paroxetine and fluvoxamine in its likelihood to cause withdrawal reactions. The syndromes closely resemble those following SSRI use.

13

How to withdraw from tranquillizers and sleeping tablets

No one can give you an infallible recipe as to how to withdraw from your tranquillizer or sleeping tablet. There are several reasons for falling back on giving general guidelines. Among these are, first, that every person is an individual with his or her own hopes, worries, personal circumstances, loves, hates and so on. In particular, each person has his or her own individual psychological and bodily makeup. Some are stoics, putting up with pain and discomfort that would reduce the average individual to desperation. At the other extreme, some, through no fault of their own, find it difficult to cope with even minor setbacks and are acutely aware of any bodily twinge or emotional swing.

Second, your feelings are subjective. That just means that no one else can feel your emotional responses – you have to communicate them. Some people are very good at this and give graphic accounts of their innermost feelings; others find this embarrassing, and stumble over finding any appropriate words.

Third, anyone reading this could be in a host of personal situations regarding their use of medication. Some are worried about starting; some ashamed to admit they need any at all. Others want some information to negotiate with their GP the choice of appropriate medication, from the point of view of effectiveness, side effects and potential withdrawal difficulties. Those who are already taking medication may worry about what will happen when they try to stop; others know that symptoms may ensue, because they have already tried to withdraw and have been assailed by alarming symptoms. Yet others, the unfortunate few, are wracked by severe withdrawal symptoms, or have protracted symptoms that they despair of ever losing.

Personal circumstances will vary immensely. One person may be surrounded by a loving set of family and friends prepared to expend time and energy supporting him through withdrawal. Another may have an abusive partner who mocks her attempts to stop taking tranquillizers and may actually prefer that the treatment not be stopped so that the taunts of 'looney' can continue. Material circumstances will also vary.

Some people can afford to take time off work when the symptoms peak; others find work takes their mind off the symptoms, and cannot afford to take a break anyway.

So, read the rest of this chapter as a set of guidelines or principles. Refer back to all the scene-setting information that I provided concerning medicines in general, the anxiety disorders and insomnia, and tranquillizers and sleeping tablets. And proceed cautiously.

Why should I stop?

It may be that you should not. If you are getting a great deal of symptom relief, and you have been taking your tranquillizer or sleeping tablet for a long time, it may be too late! This is particularly so for the elderly. They have relatively few years of lifespan left, and do not want to spend a substantial proportion of it battling with withdrawal symptoms. Most of these people have tried to stop and have developed painful, upsetting symptoms. Some, nevertheless, have never tried to stop, so cannot know whether they will have problems. After all, the chance of developing a withdrawal reaction, even in long-term users, is only about one in three. This group should dip their toes in the water and try a gradual reduction. If symptoms do come on, then at least they are aware of potential problems; if they do not, they can withdraw uneventfully.

If it is decided, perhaps in consultation with a specialist, that more harm than good would come of attempted withdrawal, there is still a need to monitor the user for the rest of her or his life. This is to detect problems that might arise from a build-up of medication effects. As people age, they become less tolerant of sedative effects and may gradually become forgetful or clumsy. In extreme cases, they are misdiagnosed as dementing. In that case, the dose must be reduced, or better, stopped.

For the vast majority of long-term users of benzodiazepines, the risks of not stopping outweigh the benefits. The benefits wear off. As I have said before, although a person taking a tranquillizer or sleeping tablet regularly may believe they still derive benefit, all the medication is really doing is suppressing withdrawal symptoms. The risks are ever present. Impairment of intellectual performance and blunting of emotions will continue. The likelihood of dependence increases steadily but is only uncovered when attempts are made to stop.

One great unknown is whether long-term damage may develop. This certainly happens with alcohol abuse (alcoholism), where the brain may shrink and only partly recover if the drinking stops. As benzodiazepines act on the brain in rather similar but more specific ways, similar brain changes may occur. Several studies have been carried out but the results are still inconclusive. Probably, there is no need to worry as long as alcohol intake is modest. But why take a risk when the benefits of long-term benzodiazepines are largely illusory?

General reasons to stop include a boost to one's self-confidence when managing to cope without a 'chemical crutch'. Self-respect returns as the ex-user meets challenge after challenge, stress after stress, without popping a pill. Psychological functioning improves on withdrawal. Appreciation of the outside world becomes heightened as the drug-induced veil is lifted. Emotions become more acute – pleasure as well as pain. The grass is greener, birds sing more loudly! Loving feelings return for family and friends and are felt properly instead of being dulled.

The bottom line is: as far as tranquillizers and sleeping tablets are concerned, almost everyone gains from stopping chronic usage.

Why start at all?

It is banal to say that the best way to deal with coming off these medications is not to start them in the first place – the old adage 'prevention is better than cure'. I hope that Chapter 10 showed that there are useful and practical alternatives to the benzodiazepines, not just other medicines but totally different methods of treatment that do not involve medication. Among the wide range is almost certainly a technique, such as relaxation or counselling, that will enable you to cope without pills. But you have to find it by trial and error.

Your doctor may try to persuade you to take medication. Thirty or so years ago, this was the accepted way of dealing with anxiety or insomnia. Sales of tranquillizers and sleeping tablets soared to unprecedented heights. But attitudes have changed. Concerted efforts by some professionals, informed lay people and the more responsible media have swung medical practice around. Most GPs are reluctant to prescribe benzodiazepines. They have realized their limited benefits and their range of side effects. The risk of dependence means that the doctor may eventually spend much more time taking his patient off a benzodiazepine than putting her on it. Also, the risk of litigation has increased – patients are ready to sue their GP if usage is not monitored properly and becomes prolonged.

Nevertheless, some GPs persist with recommending a benzodiazepine – usually elderly doctors treating elderly patients. But you do not have to accept such a recommendation – indeed, by law you have a right to refuse. You should ask the questions that I summarized at the beginning of Chapter 9, even at the risk of exasperating your doctor. It is you who is at risk, not him. Perhaps the most forceful question you can ask is, 'If I get dependent, will you arrange appropriate and intensive treatment to help me stop?'

Ask for drug information leaflets. A range is available and they usually reflect informed opinion. Argue the toss with your GP. Explain your fears of taking medications and ask what alternatives he has available. Do not let him pressurize you.

If you do change your mind before starting treatment, do let your GP know. Keep him informed of what you are taking, how much, and with what other medication. Otherwise, if something unexpected does arise, he will be in the dark and unable to advise appropriately.

If you have had problems with medication previously, make sure your doctor is reminded of this. The best predictor of withdrawal problems in the future is having had them in the past. But do not take this too far. Do not refuse all medication on principle: some medicines are helpful, at least in the short term, and not all induce dependence. Symptomatic relief for a week or two may be very useful, particularly as you wait for other ways of management to begin to take effect.

What is my present status?

If you are already on a benzodiazepine, then you need to review whether there is any suspicion that you have become dependent. Sometimes withdrawal symptoms develop even while the medication is continuing. This is because tolerance is occurring, producing a discontinuation by default. Some people know they are dependent because they have tried to taper off their medication and typical symptoms came on. But a few are so concerned about withdrawal that any symptom, perhaps a stress headache, is immediately interpreted as a withdrawal symptom. The person panics and may increase the dose unnecessarily. This is sometimes called 'pseudo-withdrawal'.

In scientific experiments of the sort that we carried out in the late 1970s, we were so concerned about this that we took elaborate precautions. We substituted dummy tablets, but neither we nor the patients (with their prior permission) were forewarned of the actual time of withdrawal. That way we could determine the true dependence status. In ordinary clinical practice, long-term users have typically tried to taper off, and developed symptoms of the type listed in Chapter 11. If that has happened then they are very likely to be dependent, and careful withdrawal is essential.

Will I cope?

Think back to how you have coped in the past. Withdrawal from tranquillizers is a pharmacological stress with two components. First, there are the bodily biochemical changes that will develop as the medicine is tapered off and leaves the body and the brain. Second, the whole process is a general stress, like bereavement, a divorce or redundancy. If you coped before with major stresses, you will pull through the process of withdrawal.

If, on the contrary, you find it difficult to manage in a crisis or if anything that happens to you is magnified into a crisis, you will need to mobilize all the family, friends and medical help you can find. Make sure that all this is in place before you embark on this withdrawal enterprise. You may even keep some forces in reserve, only calling on a particular friend, for example, when the going gets too tough.

Set up alternatives

Everyone should have learned ways of dealing with as many of the anxiety and insomnia problems as they can. There is a range here. Some, perhaps the fortunate, have long recovered from their emotional disturbance. They are 'cured', or at least nature has cured them by the passage of time and a natural healing process. They are left with a dependence on benzodiazepines that withdrawal will correct. Others are still suffering, and withdrawal will leave them anxious or insomniac, perhaps even in a worse state than before any treatment at all. They need to be able to manage that anxiety as the effects of the medication wear off, even if that medication has been only partly successful.

It is not always easy to work out where along that range a person is situated – from inherently normal but dependent, to excessively anxious but dependent as well. Therefore, everyone should assume that they will be helped by other methods of treatment. At the least, the person should be taught relaxation, attend yoga classes or learn controlled breathing.

Family and friends should be taken into the person's confidence. They can help immeasurably by instilling confidence and providing encouragement. They can help in practical ways – by doing the shopping, for example, if some agoraphobic symptoms become troublesome.

What about my GP?

Most GPs are very sympathetic to helping their patients withdraw. Many actually start the whole process. I have encountered numerous examples where a patient has changed practices, and at the initial review has been urged to consider tapering off the benzodiazepine. Only a dinosaur-type doctor is adamantly against withdrawal and insists on people continuing. If you are unfortunate enough to be saddled with an unsympathetic, unhelpful GP, ask to see another member of the practice, or if this is not possible, change your practice. If you live in a remote area with only the one local practice or a single-handed GP, insist on a referral to a psychologist or psychiatrist; have a temper tantrum if necessary. You can withdraw without your GP's help, but it is preferable that you, your family and friends all pull in the same direction.

Some GPs will, on their own initiative, review their patients' prescription records, which are now computerized, and ask to see chronic users to discuss the situation. Some send out letters suggesting methods of tapering off the benzodiazepine. Such a letter is surprisingly effective, and is often enough to motivate someone to withdraw.

Your GP may be able to refer you to additional agencies. He may know of a support group in existence nearby, and joining such a group can be very helpful. Some of these groups are run independently; others are conducted within the NHS, usually under the aegis of the local community and mental health services.

Be very cautious about being referred to the local drug-dependence services unless you have a drug addiction problem as well. These services specialize in managing drug addicts – heroin, cocaine, amphetamines and so on – and any benzodiazepine problems they deal with are in that context. Nor are alcohol services appropriate unless you recognize that you suffer from alcohol as well as benzodiazepine dependence (a not uncommon combination).

General health and lifestyle

Coming off tranquillizers is, as I repeatedly state, a stress. Any stress is best confronted when your general health is good and your lifestyle optimal.

Exercise is the number one priority. You do not have to be Olympic-level fit, but regular exercise, particularly early in the morning and later in the day, helps you relax and sleep well. You will wake up more suited to facing another day, which might otherwise become a bit of a struggle. The best exercises are those recommended for the heart – jogging, brisk walking, cycling and swimming. But do not exhaust yourself – two 20-minute periods every day is about right. Keep to a regular routine, right through the week, weekends included. It is pointless having a beneficial regime and falling to pieces on Saturday and Sunday. This means getting up at the same time – and going to bed at the same time. This helps lower anxiety and consolidates sleep rhythms.

Alcohol must be avoided. The benzodiazepines and alcohol act by similar mechanisms on the same structures in the brain. It is pointless trying to come off a benzodiazepine when all you are really doing is substituting alcohol to make up for the shortfall. If you have a problem with alcohol as well, seek help to stop drinking. When you have developed these dependencies, no level of drinking is safe. You may be able, when drug-free, to go back to mild social drinking, but don't count on it.

Caffeine is also a complication. It is present in coffee, tea and cola drinks to varying extents, and theobromine, a similar chemical, is in cocoa. Both are mild stimulants, and in excess can cause anxiety, panics and insomnia. Many people think coffee or tea has little effect on them. This may be true in some cases, but studies have shown the alerting effects of caffeine, and that it can lighten sleep and even induce anxiety. If you want to maximize your chances of stopping your tranquillizer or sleeping tablet, first taper off your coffee, tea or cola over two to three weeks. If you develop a headache, slow down the rate of withdrawal. Otherwise keep your intake to moderate limits, and keep it constant.

Cigarettes are even more difficult to give up permanently than benzodiazepines. My advice is to postpone giving up smoking until you have been free of benzodiazepines for a few months, but make it a definite target to end up with a healthy lifestyle.

Diet and fluid intake have also been regarded as important in helping withdrawal. This is often exaggerated, and faddish diets are unhelpful. A 'good' diet should be taken, with vegetables and fruit and with a minimum of junk food, although in the throes of withdrawal, the sufferer may not feel too much like shopping and cooking. Let someone else take over if you prefer. An adequate fluid intake is important, especially as your appetite for solid foods may lessen for a week or two. But be careful with sugary fluids: the fluctuations in your blood sugar may be associated with vague symptoms that may be confused with withdrawal symptoms.

This may sound like taking up the life of a Trappist monk even before you start, but you will waste a lot of time and effort if you fail and have to start all over again.

The withdrawal process

Everything is in place, you have learned relaxation techniques and you are living quietly, enjoying exercise and a good diet. You have enlisted the help of your GP, family and friends, and perhaps joined a suitable group. You are at last ready to start.

You have been warned not to stop abruptly because of the risk of epileptic fits or of becoming confused or paranoid, rather like delirium tremens (DTs). But how fast should you taper off? Remember, unless you have developed withdrawal symptoms in a previous attempt, you are more likely than not to avoid any problems, particularly if you taper. Even though long-acting medications like diazepam 'self-taper', do not take a chance – consider tapering all benzodiazepines at some rate.

Opinions differ greatly about the rate of taper. Some experts advocate a very slow rate, such as one month for every year of usage. I am not so sure. My experience was that rate of tapering and the severity of symptoms are a trade-off. You can get mild to moderate symptoms over a long time of taper, or moderate to severe symptoms over a shorter time. (For the mathematically adept: duration multiplied by severity is a constant.) This is where you have to make up your own mind. Do you want to get it all over with relatively quickly, despite bad symptoms? Alternatively, are you prepared to spin out milder symptoms over months or years because you cannot face up to a bad experience, or you have already tried unsuccessfully? The tough may opt for a short, sharp withdrawal; the less resilient may prefer a longer, gentler trip. But it may be impossible to avoid symptoms altogether by going very slowly indeed. My advice is: do not try excessively long withdrawal – you may never reach the end.

Another important observation is that the early stages of withdrawal are easier to tolerate than the later and last stages. For example, a person may reduce quite quickly from 15 mg a day of diazepam to 5 mg, and then stall as the symptoms increase from 5 mg downwards. Therefore a regular reduction may not be the most appropriate. Start fairly briskly and then slow down – but keep going.

To do this, a proportional reduction may be used, and Table 13.1 lays out an example of a *very slow* withdrawal, each reduction taking place over two to three weeks. Start with a 20 per cent reduction (one in five) over the first two to three weeks. Then reduce by a further 20 per cent each two to three weeks, until the final stages. As this is an exponential decrease, theoretically it could go on for ever, so you have to grasp the nettle at the end. Note too that this schedule takes 30–45 weeks – well over half a year in which the person's life revolves around her dose of medication and her perception of withdrawal effects.

Table 13.1 A very slow withdrawal schedule

Week	Dose
0	Starting dose (say 15 mg/day)
2–3	15 mg/day of diazepam down to 12 mg/day
4–6	12 mg/day down to 9.5 mg/day
6–9	9.5 mg/day down to 7.5 mg/day
8–12	7.5 mg/day down to 6 mg/day
10–15	6 mg/day down to 5 mg/day
12–18	5 mg/day down to 4 mg/day
14–21	4 mg/day down to 3 mg/day
16–24	3 mg/day down to 2.5 mg/day
18–27	2.5 mg/day down to 2 mg/day
20–30	2 mg/day down to 1.5 mg/day
22–33	1.5 mg/day down to 1.25 mg/day
24–36	1.25 mg/day down to 1 mg/day
26–39	1 mg/day down to 0.75 mg/day
28–42	0.75 mg/day down to 0.5 mg/day
30–45	0.5 mg/day down to 0.25 mg/day
32–48	0.25 mg/day down to 0 – stop

So let us look, in Table 13.2, at a *more rapid* schedule, with quarter reductions every two weeks. This schedule takes six months.

Table 13.2 A more rapid withdrawal schedule

Week	Dose
0	Starting dose (say 15 mg/day)
2	15 mg/day down to 11 mg/day
4	11 mg/day down to 8.5 mg/day
6	8.5 mg/day down to 6 mg/day
8	6 mg/day down to 4.75 mg/day
10	4.75 mg/day down to 3.5 mg/day
12	3.5 mg/day down to 2.5 mg/day
14	2.5 mg/day down to 2 mg/day
16	2 mg/day down to 1.5 mg/day
18	1.5 mg/day down to 1 mg/day
20	1 mg/day down to 0.75 mg/day
22	0.75 mg/day down to 0.5 mg/day
24	0.5 mg/day down to 0.25 mg/day
26	0.25 mg/day down to 0 – stop

Perhaps the *most rapid* schedule that should be considered is that shown in Table 13.3.

Table 13.3 A rapid withdrawal schedule

Week	Dose
0	Starting dose, again, as an example, 15 mg/day
2	15 mg/day down to 10 mg/day
4	10 mg/day down to 5 mg/day
6	5 mg/day down to 2.5 mg/day
8	2.5 mg/day down to 0 – stop

Eight weeks is perfectly manageable by quite a lot of patients, particularly those who have not had problems before. If symptoms start to emerge, don't panic – and don't wait for them to disappear before continuing to taper, which might take too long. Allow the symptoms to stabilize and yourself to get accustomed to them, and then continue. You will only get your life back when you finally stop taking the medication, and then some symptoms may persist for a while.

Formulations

This refers to how the medication is made available – tablets, capsules, liquids and so on. It is very unsatisfactory to try to cut up tablets using a razor blade or craft knife – quite impossible to be accurate, particularly when fractions of a tablet are sought. And capsules are little better to divide up, unless you open them up, tip out the contents and weigh out what you need on a precision balance.

The answer is a liquid preparation that you can measure out in a graduated container, as in the kitchen. Diazepam is available as an oral solution (2 mg/5 ml) and a strong oral solution (5 mg/5 ml). Make sure which you have been prescribed, and get someone else to check the dose – it's easy to make a mistake. Other medications that are available in liquid form include nitrazepam (2.5 mg/5 ml) and temazepam (10 mg/5 ml). Lorazepam is not available as a liquid, nor is zopiclone, the most widely prescribed sleeping tablet.

Changing medications

Although scientific studies have not been carried out to any extent, a firm consensus has arisen that lorazepam is much harder to withdraw from than diazepam. Many users ask for help to come off lorazepam (whose usage is less than ten per cent of diazepam's). Because of this, and the lack of a liquid preparation, it is routine to substitute diazepam for it. Now, diazepam is prescribed at an average dose of about 10 mg a day; lorazepam at about 1.5–2 mg a day – a ratio of about five to one. But for the substitution the ratio is ten to one. Thus, one needs 10 mg diazepam for every 1 mg lorazepam. The substitution should not be abrupt but take place over four weeks or so. Table 13.4 gives an example.

Table 13.4   Schedule for the substitution of diazepam for lorazepam

Week	Dose
0	1.5 mg lorazepam
1	1.0 mg lorazepam plus 5 mg diazepam
2–3	0.5 mg lorazepam plus 10 mg diazepam
4	15 mg diazepam only

This should be maintained for two to three weeks, and then the diazepam taper can start. Some people find diazepam is more sedative than lorazepam, but any sleepiness should soon wear off. As lorazepam can be prescribed up to 4 mg a day, the dose of diazepam may seem large, but clinical experience has shown that diazepam is much weaker than lorazepam in controlling withdrawal symptoms.

Other medications may need changing to diazepam using similar conversion tables. The equivalents to 10 mg diazepam are shown in Table 13.5. The diazepam is usually taken divided into three or even four fractions during the day – morning, afternoon, evening and before going to bed.

Table 13.5   Diazepam-equivalent doses

chlordiazepoxide	30 mg
loprazolam	2 mg
lormetazepam	2 mg
nitrazepam	10 mg
oxazepam	30 mg
temazepam	20 mg

Other medications – antidepressants

Naturally, when you are trying to come off a tranquillizer or sleeping tablet you are reluctant to take other medication, particularly other drugs that act on the brain, lest you should become dependent on them. That is understandable and, indeed, commendable – with one exception. Some people on tranquillizers have an underlying depressive illness. This may have been misdiagnosed because it was obscured by the more obvious anxiety or, even if detected, the wrong treatment may have been given – a sedative instead of an antidepressant. Another hazard is that some people develop a depressive illness as part of the withdrawal. Depression, as discussed in Chapter 6, is a major disorder and should be taken seriously. Psychological treatments may help minor forms, but a person with any degree of severity above that will need treating with an antidepressant. As we have seen in Chapter 12, withdrawal difficulties can follow the use of some, but not all, antidepressants. If you feel depressed, discuss this with your GP. If together you decide that an antidepressant is needed, ask him or her to select one with low withdrawal potential – fluoxetine or escitalopram, rather than fluvoxamine, venlafaxine or paroxetine. Tricyclic compounds like imipramine and amitriptyline can also be tried, but tend to produce side effects that add to the general discomfort.

If an SSRI is used, it should be started at a low dose because it can increase anxiety and insomnia during the first week. Then the full dose should be taken and maintained right through the benzodiazepine withdrawal. When you feel quite recovered, the SSRI can be tapered off using the schedule in the next chapter.

Other medications – symptomatic treatments

The mechanisms underlying withdrawal symptoms are not well understood. It is not clear why a benzodiazepine ebbing away from its receptors in the brain should give rise to so many symptoms, except that benzodiazepines act widely in the brain. Treatment for each symptom has to be on a hit-and-miss basis. Care must be taken that the symptomatic treatment does not become a problem in turn. For example, giving dihydrocodeine (DF118) for pain, if too regular and prolonged, may induce dependence of the opioid type.

Insomnia may be upsetting – the sufferer wonders if a regular sleep pattern will ever be re-established. But giving a benzodiazepine sleeping tablet or one of the 'z-drugs' (zopiclone, zolpidem or zaleplon) will only substitute dependence on one medicine for another. If insomnia persists, a non-benzodiazepine can be tried. These are generally antihistamines, such as diphenhydramine (Nytol) and promethazine (Phenergan), and are available without prescription. Some tricyclic antidepressants are also antihistaminic, and one similar medicine, trazodone, has been used, particularly in the USA, as a sleep-inducer. Melatonin and similar compounds have been advocated by some.

Some people develop severe palpitations or gastric upsets. Beta-blockers like propranolol (Inderal) may give some relief, but they are not cures.

Muscle spasms can be very upsetting. The benzodiazepines are effective muscle relaxants and can be used as such in the absence of anxiety – in people with sports injuries, for example. Some people withdrawing from a benzodiazepine are particularly plagued by unpredictable stiffness and spasms in limbs, neck, jaw and back. Headaches, again a major feature, are due to spasm in the muscles of the scalp. Jaw clenching may occur during sleep. No useful specific remedies exist as muscle relaxants may not work. Regular exercise must be resorted to.

Very occasionally, serious reactions may occur, particularly if the dose is high and withdrawal is rapid, or the person has had previous problems. Epileptic fits can be repeated and even pose a danger to life. They are usually seen in patients with previous epilepsy, but can occur for the first time during benzodiazepine withdrawal.

Psychoses with confusion, paranoid ideas or visual hallucinations may develop very occasionally. Essentially they are the equivalent to delirium tremens when withdrawing from alcohol dependence.

The treatments are anticonvulsant medication in the case of fits, and anti-psychotic medication for the psychoses. If alcohol involvement is suspected then an alcohol-withdrawal schedule must be used, together with vitamin supplements. These treatments usually work, but sometimes the dose of benzodiazepine has to be increased for a while and then tapering started again more slowly.

Withdrawal and relapse

Not everyone who has taken benzodiazepines for a long time has recovered from the illness that gave rise to the original prescription. If that is so, then discontinuing the medication can give rise to relapse symptoms, withdrawal symptoms or a mixture of both. It is important to try to work this out. Essentially, relapse is the old symptoms coming back; withdrawal is new symptoms emerging. The treatment is different: relapse needs careful assessment with a view to treating the underlying disorder, perhaps by other means; withdrawal symptoms require review of the tapering schedule.

Protracted withdrawal

This is a knotty problem. Some people who have withdrawn successfully complain of symptoms that go on and on without an end in sight. The sufferer is gradually demoralized and seeks help continually – any hope of cure, however remote, is followed up. The symptoms include anxiety and insomnia, a feeling of not 'being with it', muscle spasms and poor memory. These usually gradually resolve but may take more than a year to come down to bearable levels.

The causes of these symptoms are unclear. Some reflect psychological needs – for example, a housewife may have used her benzodiazepine dependence to hide her inadequacies as a homemaker and mother; she clings on to her symptoms to demonstrate that she is still an invalid. But these are the minority. Most patients have genuine and distressing symptoms related to some lingering abnormality in the body caused by the previous use of benzodiazepines. My assistant Sally Morton and I demonstrated this years ago when we helped several sufferers from protracted withdrawal with a single injection of the benzodiazepine antagonist, flumazenil (Anexate). Despite a few studies confirming this observation, the treatment has never been widely adopted.

Coming off sleeping tablets

Prevention

One way of avoiding becoming dependent on sleeping tablets, at least the short-acting ones, is to take them intermittently. Sleep quality varies from night to night, a bad night's sleep being followed by a better. The insomniac can usually tell when a bad one is in the offing and can take a sleeping tablet. The next night, sleep should come on without medication. The advantage of short-acting medications, such as zolpidem, is that they can be taken on an as-needed rather than an inflexible regular basis. They are so short-acting that even taken late at night, there are no residual effects ('hangover') the next day. Such intermittent use greatly reduces the risk of becoming dependent.

Withdrawing

As these medications are benzodiazepines or very similar to them, the principles of withdrawal are the same. First, the usage of sleeping tablets should be stabilized. Next, a tapering schedule like one of those above should be selected. Some people suggest taking the medication nightly for, say, a week, then every other night, every third night and so on. But this does not have any real rationale.

Because of the practical difficulties of tapering off some sleeping tablets, substitution of diazepam can be carried out as earlier. The disadvantage is that diazepam is long-acting, so may cause unwelcome sedation during the next day.

14

How to withdraw from antidepressants

I propose to follow the same structure in this chapter as in the preceding one. Of the various types of antidepressants, I shall concentrate on the tricyclics (TCAs) and the selective serotonin re-uptake inhibitors (SSRIs). The monoamine oxidase inhibitors (MAOIs) are now used quite infrequently and I will ignore them, except to say that they should be tapered under medical supervision – complications can arise.

I believe there is a fundamental difference between the use of tranquillizers and sleeping tablets on the one hand, and of antidepressants on the other. The former can provide useful symptomatic relief, at least in the short term, without too much risk. In the long term, the likelihood of dependence, with subsequent difficulty stopping, outweighs any continuing benefit. With antidepressants, the benefits are apparent both in the short and the long term. About one in three depressed patients recover completely on antidepressants, one-third show a clinically useful improvement, while the remainder respond inadequately, if at all. In the long term, any improvement is maintained, and relapse and recurrence are prevented. Thus, adverse effects with antidepressants must be judged against their undeniable benefits.

The adverse effects of tranquillizers and sleeping tablets are set against only short-term benefits. Both anti-anxiety and antidepressant drugs are associated with withdrawal effects: in the former, this follows a course of treatment with little residual benefit; in the latter, a therapeutic benefit has been conferred. With the former, the question is, 'Why continue with treatment?' With the latter, it is 'Why not continue?'

Why should I stop?

You should not stop without good reason. You have recovered from an illness that was serious, that caused you pain and even psychological agony at times, and that dominated your very being and sense of identity. The medication probably helped, although spontaneous recovery cannot be ruled out. The symptoms may not have disappeared, and are merely being kept in check by the antidepressant medicines. If you stop too soon, your symptoms are likely to return.

How do you know when it is safe to start tapering off the dose? Initial recovery from a depressive illness can be quite impressive – many symptoms go away fairly quickly. But some may linger. These include poor appetite, with loss of weight, mild insomnia and a feeling that the sparkle has not returned to your life. These are good indicators that some fraction of the depression persists. Eventually, even these symptoms fade away and the person feels fully recovered. That is the point of full recovery. About two to four months should still elapse before withdrawal is attempted.

I have repeatedly emphasized that depression is a serious disorder. It causes much symptomatic distress of a nature and to a degree beyond normal comprehension. Relief from those symptoms and impairments is not something to give up lightly. In fact, depression has a tendency to recur, especially in later life. In these individuals the antidepressant may need to be taken for many years or even for the rest of their lives. They should not stop unless advised to by their GP or psychiatrist. But most patients have a course of antidepressants over several months, perhaps up to a year, and recover from their illness. It is natural to want to stop the medication, especially as there may still be some side effects, even if muted. That is when it is important to stop in a careful manner.

What is my present status?

This is not always clear. Most patients have not tried to stop their antidepressant medication, so do not know if withdrawal symptoms will overtake them. The chances of noticeable withdrawal are much smaller when stopping an antidepressant than when stopping a tranquillizer or sleeping tablet. Consequently, the whole problem has been less studied, particularly as it has a shorter history. Although both the benzodiazepines and the TCAs were introduced around 1960, it was only with the marketing of newer antidepressants 30 years later that attention was focused on possible antidepressant withdrawal syndromes.

Because antidepressant withdrawal is less common and, on average, less severe than benzodiazepine withdrawal, the user and her or his carers and family are less aware of the problem. They find it more difficult to determine whether they are likely to have problems. The dependence types differ. With benzodiazepines, true dependence occurs, which in some people gets out of hand, with rise in dosage and abuse – so-called 'addiction'. With antidepressants, dosage increase is almost unknown, and these medicines are almost never abused. The withdrawal symptoms resemble severe rebound rather than a separate state of dependence (if you need to refresh your memory about the usage of these terms, refer back to Chapter 9).

In fact, it does not matter what terms are used, or what is the theoretical basis for the withdrawal syndromes. The important factor is whether symptoms, of the type listed in Chapter 12, are likely to occur if the antidepressant is stopped. It is impossible to say, except that if there have been difficulties on a previous attempt at withdrawal, these are likely to recur.

The upshot is that everyone taking an antidepressant should be careful to taper off their dosage. As we have seen earlier, some medications are more likely to be associated with withdrawal. Of the most commonly prescribed drugs, clomipramine (Anafranil), paroxetine (Seroxat) and venlafaxine (Efexor) are the most likely to give rise to problems. Anyone taking one of these medicines should be particularly careful.

Will I cope?

Coming off antidepressants is, by and large, much less of an ordeal than coming off benzodiazepines. Only a small fraction of patients run into the sort of problems that people stopping tranquillizers encounter. The chances of having any symptoms at all are smaller; the chances that they will be severe are smaller; the chances that they will become protracted are much smaller. There is, however, great variation between the antidepressants. The TCAs can usually be tapered down without much difficulty. This is also true of most SSRIs, except paroxetine, which often causes problems. Among the sister group of antidepressants, the SNRIs, venlafaxine is prone to cause difficulties. On withdrawing abruptly from these two drugs, about one in three people develop symptoms that last up to two weeks (again, see Chapter 12). Tapering halves this incidence but does not avoid withdrawal symptoms altogether. Therefore, if you are taking paroxetine or venlafaxine, there is an appreciable chance of – mostly mild – symptoms. If taking another antidepressant, you would be unlucky to develop really troublesome symptoms.

Set up alternatives

If you have recovered fully from your depression you should not need to set up any other ways of dealing with emotional symptoms. If you have not recovered from your depression, you should not be attempting to withdraw anyway.

What about my GP?

It is important to take advice from your GP. Unfortunately, although every GP knows about the dangers of withdrawing from benzodiazepines, some are unaware that TCAs and SSRIs can also occasionally cause problems. Psychiatrists are much more informed about this whole topic.

Assuming that your GP is knowledgeable about this potential problem, he or she should first be asked whether it is an appropriate time for you to be stopping your antidepressant. The trend over the past 20 years has been for experts to recommend longer and longer courses of treatment for depression, from three to six months and perhaps even for 12, in order to avoid premature discontinuation, with the risk of relapse. So do not be surprised if your GP is reluctant to sanction an early withdrawal from your medication. If he does, tell him that you are aware of the possibility of developing some symptoms, but that you expect these to be mild and fairly short-lived. If he insists that it is too soon to stop antidepressant medication, do not ignore his advice or insist on stopping as a matter of principle. I repeat that benzodiazepines and antidepressants are very different types of medication with different benefits and risks.

General health and lifestyle

Again, whereas these are important in setting the scene for coming off tranquillizers, they are not really a factor in stopping antidepressants. The general principles set out under this heading in the previous chapter should be followed, but as matters of hygiene, not as essential to the process of discontinuation.

The withdrawal process

Withdrawal reactions from the TCAs were uncommon because tapering off the TCA was routine practice. This procedure was not to lessen the probability and severity of potential withdrawal reactions but to make sure that the depressive illness had remitted. It was usual to lessen the dose over two to four weeks and to observe the patient, looking for early signs of relapse. If these were detected, then the original dose could be reinstated. As a by-product, the tapering also lessened the likelihood of a withdrawal reaction.

This sort of schedule is still widely used. Withdrawal reactions from TCAs are not commented on and are typically mild and short-lived. If symptoms do occur and are detected by an astute clinician, reassurance is usually all that you will need. If the symptoms are really unpleasant or persist, your doctor will probably put the dosage back up again and withdraw more slowly. This is usually sufficient.

Coming off an SSRI or an SNRI can be more of a problem, particularly with paroxetine and venlafaxine, with which most of the difficulties are associated. Again, tapering the dose over a few weeks should reduce the likelihood of any symptoms, and those that do occur should be less upsetting. Table 14.1 shows a typical withdrawal schedule from these drugs.

Table 14.1 A typical withdrawal schedule for paroxetine and venlafaxine

Week	paroxetine mg/day	venlafaxine mg/day
0	30	150
1	20	100
2	10	50
3	Stop	Stop

This is appropriate for someone who has not withdrawn from these drugs before or who has withdrawn previously without incident. If problems have occurred, either after a previous episode of depression or in attempting to withdraw in this illness, the slower taper shown in Table 14.2 is better.

Table 14.2 A slower withdrawal schedule for paroxetine and venlafaxine

Week	paroxetine mg/day	venlafaxine mg/day
0	30	150
1	25	125
2	20	100
3	15	75
4	10	50
5	5	25
6	Stop	Stop

Of course, you may be on a different initial dose – that shown in Table 14.2 is just an example. If you are coming off higher doses, proportionately longer times will be needed. If even this schedule is associated with symptoms, a slower one, over 12 weeks, should be tried. Beyond this it is doubtful whether a very slow taper will help.

If symptoms persist, one strategy is to substitute fluoxetine and slowly withdraw that. This is similar to substituting diazepam for lorazepam, discussed in Chapter 13. Substituting a TCA for an SSRI does not seem to work. Once stabilized on fluoxetine, a six-week withdrawal schedule can be tried. As fluoxetine, and especially its metabolite norfluoxetine, are very long-acting, the actual tapering will be even slower.

Formulations

Tablets and capsules are difficult to taper down and liquid preparations are preferable. Among the TCAs, amitriptyline, imipramine, lofepramine and trazodone have oral preparations, usually syrups. Among the SSRIs, citalopram, fluoxetine and paroxetine have liquid formulations, venlafaxine does not.

Changing medications

The strategy outlined above of substituting fluoxetine should be carried out keeping in mind that a 20 mg dose of fluoxetine is equivalent to:

- 10 mg escitalopram
- 20 mg paroxetine
- 20 mg citalopram
- 75 mg venlafaxine
- 100 mg sertraline
- 200 mg fluvoxamine

There is very little to guide on how to make the substitution. Doing it over a couple of weeks is sensible – see the example, using paroxetine, in Table 14.3.

Table 14.3 Substituting fluoxetine for another SSRI

Week 1	30 mg paroxetine
Week 2	20 mg paroxetine, 10 mg fluoxetine
Week 3	10 mg paroxetine, 20 mg fluoxetine
Week 4	30 mg fluoxetine

Some doctors just stop one and start the other. Very little is known of other possible substitutions – they are best avoided.

Other medications

The underlying mechanism of SSRI withdrawal is a rebound excess of the chemical serotonin in the brain and body. Symptoms of such withdrawal should be susceptible to treatment by blocking the actions of the serotonin. An example would be to stop the nausea by giving ondansetron, which blocks serotonin both in the brain and in the digestive tract. Another treatment is to give an anti-migraine treatment for headache. Less specific treatments would be a short course of sleeping tablets for the insomnia and nightmares, and anticholinergic agents, such as atropine, for the diarrhoea and sweating.

In practice these remedies are rarely prescribed as the symptoms tend to lessen within a week or two.

Second time lucky!

A description of how to stop taking an antidepressant:

Bernard is a 38-year-old landscape gardener. A year ago, at the time of some business setbacks, he developed a mixed depression and anxiety state and found it difficult to work. He was prescribed paroxetine (Seroxat) in a dose of 20 mg a day. He showed only a partial response and his GP upped the dose to 30 mg a day. After about six months Bernard felt much better, and in particular his creative abilities in designing gardens seemed to have returned. Under supervision from his GP, he started to taper off the Seroxat over four weeks. In about the second week, he developed some very disturbing electric-shock-like sensations that started at the top of his neck and went right down his spine. On one occasion these occurred while he was driving his truck, and he was concerned that his attention had been diverted from the road.

He returned to his GP, who placed him back on the 30 mg dose. His symptoms quickly subsided, and he started a much slower taper over the next three months. He still had a few symptoms, in particular dizziness, but managed to cope with them and eventually was drug free. His GP is now much less favourable towards using Seroxat and is looking into reports on all the SSRI compounds to select the one from which it is easiest to withdraw.

Withdrawal and relapse

The distinction between these two events has been repeatedly stressed. Withdrawal is the emergence of new symptoms; relapse is the re-emergence of the old. Careful description of your symptoms – by keeping a diary, for example – will help your doctor distinguish between them. The management of withdrawal will involve using one or more of the manoeuvres outlined above. These are almost always successful, so that withdrawal can be completed.

Relapse is a more serious condition. It means that the depression has not remitted but is still present. Treatment of the depression is essential, which usually means starting the medication again. Several months should elapse before tapering off is tried again.

Protracted withdrawal

Case reports have been published describing individuals who came off their antidepressant and developed what appeared to be typical SSRI withdrawal symptoms. Contrary to expectations, these symptoms persisted. Even less is understood about these protracted withdrawal syndromes than those following benzodiazepine withdrawal.

It is important to list these symptoms in detail to make sure they are not part of a relapse, particularly if they comprise general symptoms, such as anxiety and insomnia. It is also possible that stopping the antidepressant has unmasked a physical condition, so some investigations may be necessary.

Finally, some people do truly have chronic symptoms, even hypochondriasis. These may be controlled by antidepressants but re-emerge when the medication is stopped.

Antidepressants and tranquillizers together

This has been touched on in Chapter 13. The co-prescription of these medications is quite common. For example, a person suffering from depression with anxiety or from one of the anxiety disorders may be prescribed an SSRI as the main medication. Because of the high levels of anxiety, a tranquillizer may be prescribed on top to give temporary relief until the SSRI's effects become apparent. Sometimes, both medications are continued, so that the patient will need to withdraw from both a benzodiazepine and an SSRI.

The order of withdrawal is to keep using the SSRI while the benzodiazepine is withdrawn. After a pause of a few weeks, the SSRI can then be tapered off.

15

Conclusions

We have travelled a long way together. I hope that I have shown you that it is not just useful but probably essential to understand as much as possible about the mechanisms involved in withdrawal problems. Knowledge is empowerment. I reviewed with you the various types of medicines, the use of medicines and those used in psychiatric and psychological disorders. I concentrated on tranquillizers, sleeping tablets and antidepressants, by far the most extensively used.

Nonetheless, it must be admitted that we do not know much about the causes of anxiety, insomnia and depression, or about the way in which the various medications act. And in particular, we do not know much about the many factors that lead to withdrawal and discontinuation problems.

I hope that you now feel that you have the necessary knowledge to judge when to start and how to discontinue medication. There may be people and times when the medication should not be discontinued – your doctor or psychiatrist should advise you about that. But for many people, particularly with tranquillizers, long-term use is not advisable but probably not really dangerous. Conversely, with antidepressants it is important not to stop too early, otherwise the horrible symptoms of depression may come back.

Take lots of advice about stopping medication. None of us has all the answers. The more experienced I became in treating withdrawal problems, the less confident I felt in giving a firm opinion about the difficulties of withdrawal in a particular patient, and about the long-term outlook. I ended believing that the definition of an expert is someone who is acutely aware of the extent of his or her own ignorance.

Appendix
Data Sheet advice on stopping Seroxat

Seroxat (paroxetine) manufacturer's advice as approved by regulatory authority

Do not stop taking Seroxat until your doctor tells you to.

When stopping Seroxat, your doctor will help you to reduce your dose slowly over a number of weeks or months – this should help reduce the chance of withdrawal effects. One way of doing this is to gradually reduce the dose of Seroxat you take by 10 mg a week. Most people find that any symptoms on stopping Seroxat are mild and go away on their own within two weeks. For some people, these may be more severe, or go on longer.

If you get withdrawal effects when you are coming off your tablets your doctor may decide that you should come off them more slowly. If you get severe withdrawal effects when you stop taking Seroxat, please see your doctor. He or she may ask you to start taking your tablets again and come off them more slowly. It may be easier for you to take Seroxat liquid during the time that you are coming off your medicine.

If you do get withdrawal effects, you will still be able to stop Seroxat.

Possible withdrawal effects when stopping treatment

Studies show that three in ten patients notice one or more symptoms on stopping Seroxat. Some withdrawal effects on stopping occur more frequently than others. Types of symptom likely to affect up to one in ten people include:

- feeling dizzy, unsteady or off balance
- feelings like pins and needles, burning sensations and (less commonly) electric shock sensations, including in the head
- sleep disturbances (vivid dreams, nightmares, inability to sleep)
- feeling anxious
- headaches (likely to affect up to one in every 100 people)
- feeling sick (nausea)
- sweating (including night sweats)
- feeling restless or agitated
- tremor (shakiness)

- feeling confused or disorientated
- diarrhoea (loose stools)
- feeling emotional or irritable
- visual disturbances
- fluttering or pounding heartbeat (palpitations)

Please see your doctor if you are worried about withdrawal effects when stopping Seroxat.

Useful addresses

It is courteous to consult your GP first before contacting any of these organizations.

Centre for Anxiety Disorders and Trauma
Website: http://psychology.iop.kcl.ac.uk

Council for Information on Tranquillizers and Antidepressants (CITA)
(formerly **Counselling and Involuntary Tranx Addiction**)
The JDI Centre
3–11 Mersey View
Waterloo
Liverpool L22 6QA
Helpline: 0151 932 0102 (Monday to Friday, weekends, bank holidays, 10 a.m. to 1 p.m.)
Website: www.citawithdrawal.org.uk

Depression Alliance
212 Spitfire Studios
63–71 Collier Street
London N1 9BE
Tel. (request for information pack only): 0845 123 2320
Website: www.depressionalliance.org

Drugscope
Tel.: 0870 774 3682
Website: www.drugscope.org.uk

Mind (National Association of Mental Health)
15–19 Broadway
London E15 4BQ
Tel.: 020 8519 2122
Website: www.mind.org.uk

Release
388 Old Street
London EC1V 9LT
Helpline: 0845 4500 215

Samaritans
Helpline: 08457 90 90 90 (24 hours, every day)
Website: www.samaritans.org

Sane
First Floor, Cityside House
40 Adler Street
London E1 1EE
SANEline: 0845 767 8000 (1 p.m. to 11 p.m., every day)

Turning Point
Standon House
21 Mansell Street
London E1 8AA
Tel.: 020 7481 7600
Website: www.turning-point.co.uk

Further reading

Ashton, Heather, *Benzodiazepines: how they work and how to withdraw*, on <http://www.benzo.org.uk/manual/index.htm>.

McAllister-Williams, Hamish, articles on *Anxiety Disorders* and *Depression*, on <http://www.netdoctor.co.uk/diseases/>.

Mental Health Foundation, articles on *Anxiety* and *Depression*, on <http://www.mentalhealth.org.uk/information/mental-health-a-z/>.

National Institute for Health and Clinical Excellence (NICE), *Depression: management of depression in primary and secondary care* (Clinical guideline 23). London: NICE, 2004.

NHS Direct, articles on *Depression* and *Anxiety*, on <http://www.nhsdirect.nhs.uk/encyclopaedia/a-z/>.

Tighe, James, *Anxiety disorders*, on <http://www.bbc.co.uk/health/conditions/mental_health/disorders_anxiety.shtml>.

Index